THE MAN iN THE CEILING

entirely written
and illustrated by

Jules Feiffer

Text and pictures copyright © 1993 by Jules Feiffer
All rights reserved
Library of Congress catalog card number: 92-59953
Designed by Cynthia Krupat
First edition, 1993
Tenth printing, 1999

For Halley

THE MAN IN THE CEILING

Jimmy goes camping with his father. Not in real life; this is a comic book. Jimmy's father wears a broad-brimmed hat with a flat crown and a safari jacket with pockets for everything: a map, a compass, a flashlight, fishhooks. The way Jimmy draws him, he looks like Indiana Jones.

Jimmy's father is an expert woodsman. Not in real life, but in the comic book. He guides Jimmy through the dense forest by light touches on the shoulder. When he touches his left shoulder, Jimmy goes left; when he touches his right shoulder, Jimmy goes right. His father's touches feel good to Jimmy. Bears are in these woods. Also snakes. "Doin' fine, kiddo," says his father, who doesn't talk much.

CHAPTER 1

Sometimes Jimmy imagined his father carrying a canoe on his shoulder and sometimes not. The trouble Jimmy had with the canoe idea was that, if they were trekking through these thick woods, wasn't the canoe likely to bang into trees, knocking his father off balance, possibly into a swamp with live alligators? Actually, not a bad idea. Or this: What if the canoe got tangled in the branches of a tree, high off the ground, and just hung there? Jimmy liked that even better than the alligator idea. He had to laugh as he drew it.

Jimmy's father called him "kiddo" in the stories that Jimmy made up. Jimmy didn't entirely mind that his actual father didn't call him "kiddo" or take him camping in the woods. First of all, it wouldn't have been as much fun, and second, his father was too busy and overworked to take him camping in the woods. The word Jimmy heard most about his father was "overworked." The way his mother said it, "overworked" sounded important, even a little mysterious, something that perhaps Jimmy should grow up to be.

Father always brought home a pile of papers from the aircraft plant where he overworked, not far from where Jimmy and his family lived in Upper Montclair. "Don't touch my papers," Father said every time, although neither Jimmy nor his mother or sisters ever dreamed of going near his papers. Just to look at them was enough to know that these were papers not meant to be touched. They had *equations*. Father might just as well have said, "Don't touch my atom bomb." Why in the world did he think that Jimmy would be tempted?

At times, Jimmy drew on the floor just behind the metal desk where Father worked on his papers. It made him feel that they were colleagues of sorts, two men— the only two in the family—busily making mysterious marks on sheets of paper. I say "mysterious" because Father no more understood Jimmy's drawings than Jimmy understood Father's equations. Jimmy felt self-conscious drawing with Father nearby. He pretended that Father was not really working on his equations but watching Jimmy out of the corner of his eye. So every line Jimmy drew was a line for Father. Not that Father got it. Mother sometimes got it, but she was an artist herself, so it was to be expected. His older sister, Lisi, got it, but she was Jimmy's biggest fan, so big deal! But Father? Father never got it.

The effort it took to make a good Indiana Jones drawing made Jimmy grunt. The grunts were for Father's benefit. Jimmy hoped that just once Father would look up and say, "Not as easy as it looks, right, kiddo?" But Father didn't hear Jimmy's grunts. He was lost in thought over his equations. Sometimes Jimmy invented things to say to get his attention. Like one time he asked, "If you love, I mean really love your job, isn't it fair that you should be paid less?"

This was on his mind because, while he intended to grow up to draw cartoons (which he loved), still and all, he had to make money to support a family. So the question was not frivolous. Jimmy continued: "If a job is fun, maybe you shouldn't get paid—or O.K., paid, but food and carfare and something for the movies. I mean, shouldn't you get paid more for a job you hate?"

Father's pen hand stopped jotting down numbers. His eyes lost focus and his face took on a funny, pinched look. It was as if he were trying to translate Jimmy's words into his own native tongue. But that couldn't be, because Father was born in Columbus, Ohio.

"Don't bother your father, he's busy," said Jimmy's mother, who seemed never to be there except to stop Jimmy from bothering his father. At other times she said, "Don't bother your father, he's resting," which simply wasn't true. Jimmy never saw Father rest. Even asleep, he looked like it was a job.

So, between a busy father and a resting father (as if!), Jimmy chose to create a father he *could* bother. And this father—his Indiana Jones of a father—was so ideal that Jimmy wouldn't have wanted his actual father to be like that. It would confuse things. He didn't mind sharing his actual father with his two sisters, Lisi and Susu, but his Indiana Jones of a father? No way!

CHAPTER 2

Jimmy's older sister, Lisi, was close to Father in a way that Jimmy wasn't because Lisi watched baseball with Father. Jimmy didn't like baseball, and that was why he and Father weren't close and never would be. Because what else does a father do with a son but talk baseball and watch and play baseball? And talking to Jimmy about baseball was a waste of time. If Father wanted to talk to Jimmy about superheroes, that might lead to real companionship, but Jimmy knew nothing about baseball. Besides, he had no talent for the game.

So Father had no one to shag flies with or pitch to or give advice on how to play the game. Since he couldn't advise Jimmy, he advised the players on the TV screen and shared that advice with Lisi. "What you wanna do in a spot like this—two men on, no one out—is advance the base runners to second and third, which means the batter bunts, which is a certain out but puts your two

base runners in scoring position with two outs left to bring 'em home, except in this case, with Dombrowski, a .342 hitter, at the plate, and Mertz, the pitcher, up next (Mertz can't hit his weight), Dombrowski is sure not to bunt. He's likely to fake a bunt to fool the pitcher, but take a tip from your old man, he'll hit away, which is why the infield is in, to play the bunt just in case, but the outfield is playing deep, waiting for the long ball." This kind of talk, which Lisi appeared to understand, sounded like equations to Jimmy.

Don't get me wrong about Father. It's not that he didn't like Jimmy, he just didn't have a clue as to what he was about. He wanted a son he could share batting averages and pitching percentages with. Instead, he got Jimmy. He tried to make the best of it. I mean, he was still a father, he still paid for Jimmy's food and clothes and Christmas and birthday presents. He was a good father in those ways. And he still managed to find things to say to Jimmy, like "Do you have to leave your pictures lying all over the floor?" or "Could you lower that TV down to a scream?" Or sometimes more hurtful things, like "Are you still batting zero for ninety? Ha-ha."

Jimmy didn't think Father was out to hurt him deliberately. He just didn't know any other way to behave with a son who drew pictures. Jimmy left the pictures that Father complained about all over the floor on purpose. He hoped that Father would come upon them as if they were there by accident, and pick up the first page and then go on to the next ten or fifteen pages and be flabbergasted. "I can't believe a boy of ten and a half could have drawn *this!*" were the words Jimmy imagined Father saying. He never said them.

His Indiana Jones of a father would have said those words. His Indiana Jones of a father was always encouraging.

And Jimmy, who was not named Jimmy in the comic he made up, but Bob, leaped off the cliff . . .

And his Indiana Jones of a father caught him.

"He reminds me a little of your brother, Lester," Father had said to Mother more than once in regard to Jimmy. This was not a nice thing to say. Father was not a fan of Mother's brother, Lester. I'll tell you about that later. What's important to tell you now is Mother's response because that will explain a little about Mother. Her response was, "Uh-huh, I'd better finish, it's getting late."

Whatever it was she had to finish, and there are a million things mothers have to finish (and Jimmy's mother worked, so she could claim she had to finish a million and one things), she always needed to finish them when Father brought up Jimmy. Mother didn't want to talk to Father about Jimmy. Jimmy was *hers*, Lisi was *his*. Father and Lisi watched ball games together, played

Scrabble together, laughed at the jokes Mother didn't get together. But Jimmy was hers, and if she didn't understand Jimmy either, she didn't understand him in a way that was more sympathetic than Father's way. Mother generally laughed off what she didn't understand. She laughed off much about Jimmy, but she laughed in his favor.

CHAPTER 3

One day Jimmy came up from the basement (his secret place to draw comics) and found Lisi showing some of his really old stuff to Father. Stuff that he had drawn more than a month ago and was ashamed of. Lisi was pointing to a picture. "That's you," she said. And Father responded, "That's not me," and Lisi said, "Yes, it is, it looks just like you."

Now, maybe it did and maybe it didn't, but this was a dumb thing to say to Father. Particularly since Lisi was trying to prove to him what she and Mother knew but not Father: that Jimmy was a really good artist. This was not the way to go about it. Father squinted at Jimmy's comic. He knew what he looked like, and he didn't look like that boob in a safari jacket. "My nose is *not* that big." Father snorted. "Where's my chin?"

Jimmy was crushed. First of all, the only reason Lisi knew that the Indiana Jones character was a made-up version of Father was that she tricked it out of him. She tricked all his secrets out of him, which is what he most disliked about Lisi, whom he was crazy about otherwise —except for her bossiness, which you'll hear about in the next chapter.

It was a mistake to tell Lisi anything. She wasn't supposed to know about Indiana Jones. No one was supposed to know except Father, who was supposed to discover it by himself when he picked up the drawings and said, "Do you have to leave your pictures all over the— Hey, what's this? This looks just like me! Hey, and I'm Indiana Jones!"

But Lisi spoiled it, because nobody thinks a drawing looks like him if somebody else points it out. They have to see it for themselves. That was one of Jimmy's rules. Jimmy could have killed Lisi.

Indiana Jones was ruined as a comics character. That message was loud and clear. He had been a good hero, possibly a great hero. (The way he shoved a piece of driftwood into the jaws of a charging crocodile!)

But Lisi had exposed Jimmy. Father had snorted. Snorted! Jimmy replayed the scene in his head a dozen times over and died every time. Indiana had to go. Be replaced. But who could possibly replace Indiana Jones?

Jimmy brooded over that question for the next two afternoons. He behaved more rudely than usual to his little sister, Susu.

"Play with me, Jimmy."

"Go away, you pest."

Susu was five. She thought "Go away, you pest" was a joke. However rude Jimmy was to her, she took it as a joke. Half the time it was. Half the time it wasn't. This time it wasn't. But that didn't change things with Susu. She was completely gaga over her big brother.

"Play with me, Jimmy."

"Go away or I'll pull your teeth out one by one."

"Play with me, Jimmy."

But Susu had to wait.

"Jimmy, I want you to go to the store for me."

Mother had to wait.

"Now where did that boy disappear to this time?"

Homework had to wait. Jimmy needed a new hero. A hero untainted by the judgment of Lisi and Father. A hero they would never get a glimpse of. Or if they did in fifty years or so, after Jimmy was old and maybe dead, then they'd think: "If we had only known when he was ten and a half that he could create such a hero!"

He tried everything, but nothing worked. He felt worse

and worse, small and useless. Bored and without anything better to do, Jimmy drew himself small and useless. A light bulb turned on in his head the way it does in comics when a character gets an idea. He drew a black mask and a cape on his small and useless character. It didn't look right. He turned the mask into a hood. He looked on the character he had created and was thrilled. He had come up with, potentially, his greatest hero yet. So small and useless in appearance that villains thought they could kill him easily. They could trap him, torture him, run him over in cars, even tanks. But no one, *no one*, could defeat *Mini-Man*!

MINI MAN
The Smallest man alive!
BART BOYLE, ADVENTURER HAS LEARNED THE ANCIENT MAGIC OF THE ANCESTER FROM HIS ANCIENT CHINESE MASTER. NOW HE AIDS THE DOWN-TRODDEN AND OPRESSED FOR HE IS... MINI MAN
BUT SO SMALL NO CRIM-INAL CAN CATCH HIM AND NO CRIME WILL GO UN-REVENGE
Jimmy
written and illustrated by Jibbell

NEXT NIGHT
WONDER IF MY DISGUISE WILL FOOL THE BLACK BA—
A GRIP OF STEEL!
DIE!
WHA-
BEFORE HE IS CH-OKED BART UTTERS THE ANCIENT CHINESE WORDS HIS MASTER TAUGHT HIM!
MING YING
BART HAS SHRUNK TO THE SIZE OF A TINY PEBBLE FOR HE HAS TRANSFORMED TO ...MAN!
WHAT TH—
I'LL TEACH YOU TO PICK ON GIRLS!

CHAPTER 4

"Come hither, my slave!" commanded Lisi.

"I'm not your slave!" Jimmy snapped.

"Don't talk back to me, slave!" Lisi snapped back. Lisi's snaps easily outsnapped Jimmy's snaps.

She was playing "Slave Empress," a game that everyone but Lisi got tired of about a year ago. But when Lisi chose to play with Jimmy and Susu, they played. And when she chose to play "Slave Empress," they played that. And when she chose to play "Warrior Queen," they played that. In addition, they played "Cat Woman," "Oprah," "Roseanne," and "Jane of the Jungle" (Tarzan was dead, killed by white hunters; his death was avenged by Jane many times over in every room of the house).

"You're my courtier," Lisi announced. She stood barefoot on her parents' bed, draped in a colorful array of new curtains that had yet to be hung, although they'd been lying around for weeks. ("I'll get to it," Mother said when she noticed the curtains, apparently for the first time, on arising each morning.)

"I'm the Empress. You're my courtier. You must bow to me."

Because they were too lowly, Jimmy and Susu were not permitted on the bed where Lisi stood. "What's a courtier?" said Jimmy, who hated to admit to his sister that she understood words he didn't.

"A servant," Lisi said, as if he really was one.

"I'm not a servant. I'm a Knight of the Round Table!"

"All the Empress's subjects are her servants."

Jimmy was backed into the same corner he found himself in every time with Lisi. Whether she was playing the part of empress or rock star or host of her own TV talk show, Jimmy lost all his arguments with her.

For example, if he started out believing that he knew as much about—oh, say, which was a better way to die, in a car crash or a plane crash. Then he and Lisi got into this discussion about which way: car crash or plane crash? The discussion always led to an argument: "It's better in a car," said Jimmy, "because you crash and, bang! it's over, but if you're in a plane you're falling and falling and everyone's screaming, 'Let me out of here!' and you can't jump out at the last second like in a car and save yourself."

Lisi had a special look that Jimmy particularly hated. This was the look that told him he was demented. When she had that look, she spoke to him as if she were talking to a person who was not quite normal. "What if you don't get killed but get burned and crippled and sit in a wheel-chair for the rest of your life with tubes and plastic bags sticking out of every part of your body and your head is twisted this way and your body is twisted that way and when you try to talk you grunt, 'Uhhh-uhhh.' That's what happens in a car crash!"

Jimmy was left with no ground to stand on. Lisi argued with such conviction that he didn't have a chance. He felt trapped, wrong, and stupid. But in his heart of hearts he believed that he was smart, right, and a lousy arguer.

CHAPTER 5

"Draw me!" pleaded Susu.

"Go away, pest." This was something Jimmy said to Susu so often that he didn't even know he said it. He was deep into an episode of *Mini-Man*. Mini-Man's archrival and nemesis, Molten-Man (the hottest man alive, one touch and you went up in flames), was setting fire to the town's school. Children could burn up alive! Only Mini-Man could stop this dastardly scheme. And Susu interrupts to have her portrait drawn! The nerve of her! The last thing in the world Jimmy was interested in was drawing Susu—or anyone from real life. The whole point to drawing was to make it up out of your own imagination. Even Father as Indiana Jones was made up. Father didn't say "Draw me" to Jimmy. He would never have said it. And Jimmy would never have done it, because why be an artist if you are going to waste your talent drawing what was there in front of your nose? It didn't make sense.

Another point that Jimmy didn't much like to think about: drawing from real life was harder than drawing from imagination. Drawing a tree from real life (or a car or a dog) had never yet turned out the way Jimmy intended. The real tree, car, or dog looked distressingly different from what he drew. But when he drew a tree without looking at one, who was to say it wasn't a perfect picture of the tree he had in mind? And the same for cars and dogs.

"What's that you're drawing?" Lisi said, in a voice that meant "Gotcha!" Where did she come from? Susu had vanished, and as if by magic, Lisi appeared in her place.

No one bothered Mother, the other artist in the family. Mother had her own special place to work, a place she called her "sanctum sanctorum," which meant that no one dared go there and say "Draw me" or "What's that you're drawing?" to her. Mother was a fashion designer, which was a lot less important in Jimmy's eyes than drawing superheroes, but he could be interrupted and not her. It was so unfair!

It hurt Lisi's feelings that Jimmy didn't show her his comics anymore. Her very presence, her intimidating manner, her penetrating stare made more than clear what she intended him to do. But Jimmy was not about to risk a humiliating repeat of the Indiana Jones episode ("My nose is not that big. Where's my chin?"). And so Lisi's feelings were hurt.

Hurting Lisi's feelings was not a good idea. It could lead to—well, you'll soon see what it could lead to. No one in his right mind would want to end up there.

"I couldn't care less if you showed me your stupid drawing—go get me a chocolate-chip cookie and a glass of milk."

Now, this remark of Lisi's was in code. Jimmy understood the code, but you won't, so I'll decipher it for you. What Lisi *really* said was: "You are going to show me your drawings again or I will make your life a living curse, and you know I'm the girl who can do it."

Jimmy did a swift strategy study: "If I hide my drawing, go to the kitchen, and get her the stupid cookie and milk, I'll be back here in a minute and she'll have to go away. If I don't—which by rights I shouldn't . . ." Inwardly, he shuddered at the consequences. Outwardly, he sighed deeply to demonstrate to Lisi the sacrifice he was making out of the goodness of his heart. Then he got up very slowly, so that she wouldn't think he was scared of her, and started for the kitchen.

"Play with me, Jimmy," said Susu, who had been waiting in the kitchen for this moment.

"I'm busy," said Jimmy, opening the refrigerator door.

"Play with me, Jimmy."

"Will you go away?" Jimmy had to half empty out the top shelf of the refrigerator to get to the milk.

"I'm going to disturb Mother if you don't play with me," said Susu.

Now, "disturb Mother" was no threat to be taken lightly. Mother's sanctum sanctorum was in a tiny, cluttered corner squeezed into the attic. Mother was tiny, the drawing table on which she designed her fashions was tiny. The two of them fit, without an inch to spare, just under the attic eaves. Mother was the most easygoing mother in the world, except when she was disturbed in her sanctum sanctorum. Jimmy was trapped.

He was able to deal with only one threat at a time. The threat facing him at the moment (Susu) caused him to forget the threat waiting for milk and a chocolate-chip cookie in the living room. He slammed shut the door of the refrigerator. "One story!" he snarled. Susu nodded in

ecstasy. She was used to not getting her way, just as Lisi was used to the opposite.

Jimmy began the story as he always did: "Once upon a time, there was a tricky little bear named . . ." He paused, waiting for Susu to give the name.

"Tricky Duck!" shouted Susu. She always supplied the wrong name.

"No. Once upon a time, there was a tricky little bear named—um . . ." He paused again, pretending to forget.

"Tricky Mouse!" cried Susu.

"No. No," corrected Jimmy. "Once upon a time, there was a tricky little bear named . . ." Jimmy waited. He giggled inside. He knew Susu was giggling inside, too, but she pretended to be thinking.

"Tricky Horse?" hinted Jimmy.

"No."

"Tricky Cat?" hinted Jimmy.

"No."

"Tricky *Bear*!" screamed Jimmy.

"JIMMY, WHERE ARE YOU?"

Jimmy might have forgotten Lisi and the milk and the cookie, but Lisi didn't forget.

Suddenly she was there, Lisi in the kitchen. Staring at Jimmy and Susu so hard, so fiercely, so violently, that before she said or did anything, Jimmy turned white and Susu began to cry.

Jimmy was caught like a small animal in the blinding headlights of Lisi's rage, the very thing he had gone for the milk and cookie to avoid. Lisi's temper was—there is no other word for it—terrifying. It terrified her as well, but she was not in charge of it, it was in charge of her. It took her over when it struck and didn't release her until its force was spent—and she was spent, and everyone within hearing distance was bled dry.

Now, I could take up the next five pages telling you what Lisi said, and it would be printed in capital letters to show how loud she said it, but you'd get bored reading the same lines over and over, so what's the point? However, I'll give you some examples: "**I ASKED YOU FOR ONE SIMPLE FAVOR, AFTER ALL THE FAVORS I DO FOR YOU!**" and "**YOU ARE SO**

UNFAIR!'' and "YOU DON'T CARE ABOUT ANYONE BUT YOURSELF!'' and "YOU ARE SO SELFISH I CANNOT BELIEVE IT! I CAN-NOT BELIEVE IT! I CANNOT BELIEVE IT!'' There'd have to be one whole page of I CANNOT BE-LIEVE ITs. Followed by another page or two of HOW DARE YOUs. After all that, you'd have a very bad impression of Lisi, which would be the wrong impression because, except for her temper, which, as you know, she had no control over, she was as kind and warmhearted a twelve-year-old as you'd find anywhere.

She loved her family, especially her father and brother. She had a lot of friends, a lot more than Jimmy. She wrote letters to relatives and thank-you notes for presents. She encouraged Jimmy in his drawing more than anyone else did, including Mother. She might have been one of the three or four nicest people in the world if it weren't for that unbelievable temper.

Mother came flying downstairs from her sanctum sanc-torum, her teeth clenched, her eyes blazing. "I would like to know the reason for this disturbance." She held a paintbrush in one hand and a tube of blue watercolor in the other. Her hands were as clenched as her teeth, which was not a good idea: the tube of blue watercolor oozed out onto her fingers and down her pants leg. "I'm waiting to hear the reason for this disturbance." Mother's hands were never not stained with watercolor, and the same can be said of all but her best clothes. "Is no one going to

tell me what this disturbance is all about?" It's hard to use the word "disturbance" so many times in a row without beginning to sound foolish. Particularly if no one responds.

Unlike Lisi, Mother was a calm person, slow to anger and quick to recover. So as Lisi—who had not heard a word she said—continued to cry out, "**I ASKED YOU FOR ONE SIMPLE FAVOR,**" Mother switched her sights to Jimmy.

"Jimmy, apologize to Lisi."

Jimmy was shocked at Mother. Lisi was the one causing the disturbance! He turned away from the unfairness of it all, leaving Mother no one to face but Lisi. "Jimmy apologizes, Lisi."

This piece of flimflam had no more effect on Lisi than her use of the word "disturbance," so Mother switched tactics once again. "Let's all try to be a little more generous to each other, starting right now, shall we?"

"Generous" was one of the words Mother used a lot, like "disturbance." It meant different things depending on how she used it. And it was up to the children to figure it out. She might mean "generous" as in (1) "a generous helping of ice cream," or (2) "Be generous to the homeless," or (3) "I'm feeling generous, so you can stay up late tonight."

"Generous" might mean "large" or "kind" or "good," or even "stupid," as in "You're too generous for your own good."

If I were to illustrate the end of this chapter, which I don't have time for because of the more important drawings I have to do later in this book, the illustration would be of Lisi sitting at the kitchen table drinking a tall glass of milk and eating a chocolate-chip cookie which Jimmy finally got for her so that the fight could be over. Lisi would look quite pleased with the world. In the background, I'd draw Jimmy and Susu in a state of shock, the way you look after you've been in a car crash and no one got killed but you don't know why. Mother would not be in the drawing. She ran back to her sanctum sanctorum too fast.

CHAPTER 6

Susu had no interest in superheroes, even one as unusual as Mini-Man. So Jimmy made up stories for her that were more appropriate to her age level. And these were the Tricky Bear stories. It would be nice to say that Jimmy made them up out of the goodness of his heart, but that would not be true. The reason he told Susu stories was to get rid of her.

He had tried every other way to get rid of her. First, he tried to hurt her feelings. This was not easy. Susu was so crazy about Jimmy that no matter how hard he worked to be awful to her she thought he was kidding. It took a lot of time—more time than it would have taken to play with her—to insult Susu. And it always backfired. Because it sent her crying upstairs to the sanctum sanctorum and brought Mother flying downstairs to say, "I just hope no one ever treats you as ungenerously as you treat Susu."

Then Mother was gone and Jimmy was left to play with Susu for the rest of his life (or so it seemed).

Jimmy was not always ungenerous. Although telling Tricky Bear stories started out as a duty (one long, stupid story and Jimmy could get back to his comics), to his surprise he'd get caught up in the story and begin enjoying himself. As a matter of pride, he kept that a secret.

I will have to draw Tricky Bear for you because, even though Jimmy created him, he wouldn't dream of drawing him. It scared him that any Tricky Bear he tried to draw wouldn't live up to the one in Susu's imagination. Susu must have felt the same way. In any case, she never asked.

The character of Tricky Bear was inspired by Winnie-the-Pooh—the one from the Walt Disney cartoons, not the book. Jimmy planned to draw for the Walt Disney Studio someday. He wanted to create his own characters, like Mini-Man. He liked to imagine Mini-Man on the screen, drawn in the Disney style instead of his own style, which wasn't good enough yet. By the time he was twenty-one, Jimmy was sure it would be.

It was the one thing in his childhood he was sure of: that one day, surely before he reached his father's age, he would be a great cartoonist. That knowledge was Jimmy's best-kept secret. He never talked to anyone about it, not even Lisi, who managed sooner or later to get all his secrets out of him. But not the one about being a great cartoonist.

CHAPTER 7

As Jimmy saw it, he had no choice but to grow up to be a great cartoonist. Only that would make up for the awful burden he bore in the present. Because, in every way that counted, Jimmy was a flop as a boy.

It is nearly impossible to be a successful boy in America if you can't play ball. Jimmy could throw a little, but the ball wouldn't go very far, and where it went was never where he aimed it. It was either higher or lower, and nowhere near where he intended when he wound up to pitch. He looked good winding up. TV taught him how: how to stand, how to wind up, how to throw, how to run bases, and how to look good running bases, with his head down and his shoulders high and his arms pumping away, tight in on his body instead of waving in the air like a windmill, which would have been his way if he hadn't watched TV and learned how.

Not that Jimmy ever got a chance to run bases. He was

almost never picked for the team. No one wanted him. Not only couldn't he throw a ball, he couldn't hit and he couldn't catch, either. He was a triple non-threat.

Don't take my word for it: I'll show you. Here's Jimmy out in right field.

Now, when other kids are out in the field and a fly ball comes their way and they cry, "I got it, I got it!" they get it. Now here's Jimmy. A fly ball is coming his way.

He knows what to say, all right: "I got it, I got it!" That is absolutely correct, but only if you get it. That was the part Jimmy didn't know how to do. He did the shouting part fine, but he never caught the ball. He caught nearly the ball. He caught almost the ball. He caught all the air and floating specks of dirt around the ball. Just not the ball.

Jimmy didn't have patience for what he wasn't good at. If he couldn't learn a skill without going through a lot of effort and pain and humiliation, then what was the point? Why bother? Why bother with math, which he wasn't good at? Why bother with social studies?

Jimmy thought the world was divided into kids who picked up on things fast and kids who didn't. Kids whose hands were raised in class every two minutes and kids, like Jimmy, who, even when they were sure of the answer, weren't *that* sure. Some kids could master any new game in two minutes. Jimmy wasn't one of them. Some kids were what his teachers called "natural leaders." They took charge. They knew something about everything.

Jimmy knew he was bright, but still and all, he seemed to know less about most things than he should have. The reason was, he didn't pay attention. He didn't pay attention because he was daydreaming. As he daydreamed, he drew in the margins of the pages of his loose-leaf book —and sometimes when he got carried away, he even drew all over his homework. His teachers and everyone else told him that if he stopped drawing in class he'd "retain" more. He tried that. It didn't work. He didn't "retain" anything. Not the lesson, not his daydreams. He went blank. He floated away inside himself.

His teachers had one opinion about Jimmy, and they'd been writing it on reports since the first grade: "Jimmy is bright and imaginative, but he doesn't apply himself." You cannot believe how off the mark these reports were. Jimmy did apply himself. But to what *he*, not they, thought was important.

When his mother was struggling with him over his math and said, "You made that mistake last time and the time before, you've got to pay attention," Jimmy's secret thought was: "Multiplication isn't important to a great cartoonist."

When his father lost his patience because Jimmy's reading skills were below grade level and said, "I've had it with you, young man," and walked out of the room and went into his den and drank a beer, Jimmy's secret thought was: "I'll remind him of this day when I'm a great cartoonist."

Jimmy envied his mother her sanctum sanctorum. He liked to go up to the attic and hang out under the eaves when she wasn't around. He'd sit at her drawing table and look over her fashion sketches (which he couldn't make head or tail of) and imagine drawing something really good like *Mini-Man* in that very space, on that very table. He got the idea from his mother's studio for his own sanctum sanctorum, which was a corner of the laundry room in the cellar, but wasn't nearly as nice and smelled of soap.

Jimmy came up with his own name for his sanctum sanctorum. He made a sign for the cellar door that read:

One night, he screwed up his courage and announced to the family at the dinner table, "When I'm in my inner sanctum, no one can disturb me." As it happened, his mother and Lisi were having an argument about orthodontia and didn't hear him.

CHAPTER 8

The kids in Jimmy's school knew he drew comics because that's what he did in class, and very little else. He drew cartoons at recess and, when he got lucky, even in gym. "Let's see, Jimmy, let's see," nudged his classmates, because they were curious about any kid who got away with spending all that time in school doing what he liked. But the only kid to be granted permission to actually see Jimmy's comics was Charley Beemer. The reason was clear: Charley Beemer was royalty. Lisi may have acted like royalty at home, but outside she couldn't get away with it. On the other hand, Charley Beemer was royalty anywhere he happened to be: at home, in school (even in the classroom!), and, most of all, on the ball field.

First of all, Charley Beemer was tall for his age (which was almost twelve), as blond and handsome as the prince in fairy tales, and a good student (but not great, not so smart that the other guys had a reason to dislike him).

And he had a sensational smile. When Charley Beemer smiled, everyone around him smiled.

Whatever Charley did, that's what everyone else did. Not that Charley made them; they just wanted to. If Charley said, "Let's go to a movie," all the kids in his crowd, whatever else they were doing, wanted to stop and go to a movie. And the movie they wanted to see was the one Charley wanted to see. And the row they wanted to sit in was the exact row Charley had chosen. And this was true in regard to the size of the bag of popcorn and the size and the kind of soda and whether they talked or shut up in the movie and which route they took on the way home. Charley never seemed to be leading or imposing his will. It was just that the decisions the boys in Charley's crowd came to of their own free will were the same decisions that Charley had arrived at a second or two earlier.

Jimmy was not part of Charley's crowd. He was too young. And looked younger. And he acted even younger

than he looked around Charley and his crowd. And more important than any of that, he couldn't play ball.

But he loved to watch Charley play because Charley played like a superhero. He didn't run, he glided. He didn't hit, he walloped. He didn't catch balls; they simply appeared, like magic, in his glove. Nothing Charley did looked as if it required effort.

And he was a nice guy. That was what was so hard to believe: that anyone as good as Charley, as admired as Charley, as super a star as Charley, wasn't stuck up.

Charley had an incredible sense of humor—not that

he made jokes, but he loved jokes, anyone's jokes. And he turned all sorts of stories that weren't jokes into jokes. He laughed, and suddenly a boring story from one of his pals about forgetting a book in the school library and going back for it but it was too late, the library was closed—a story *that* boring would bring a laugh out of Charley Beemer so full of delight that the storyteller had to believe that he had told one of the ten best stories of the year.

Charley, who was better than any kid at just about anything, made the kids around him feel that they were almost as good as he was. It wasn't anything he said or did. It was simply his presence. That's why he was royalty.

Charley Beemer kept Jimmy around for one reason: Jimmy could draw and Charley couldn't. One more nice thing about Charley Beemer was that when someone was better at something than he was he didn't get jealous, he got interested. He got curious. How was it possible for Jimmy, who was a year and a half younger, to draw such good superheroes? "How do you do it, from the head down or the feet up?"

"From the face out," Jimmy explained. He demonstrated how he first penciled in the eyebrows and eyes of a character, then the nose and mouth. "The eyebrows and the mouth are the most important, because that's how you get the expression, like the eyebrows are up and the mouth is down if you're sad, but the eyebrows are down and the mouth is down if you're mad." Jimmy drew quickly to show Charley what he meant, and Charley was astounded. Then Jimmy outlined the head around the features, including the hair (or the hood; a lot of superheroes wore hoods). Then he sketched in the body, which was the part Charley enjoyed most, because Jimmy's specialty was action poses and Charley loved action.

Strange as it may seem, Jimmy, who was terrible at sports, was great at drawing action: superheroes running, jumping, shooting, and especially zapping bad guys with their oversized fists, which were encased in thick, smudgy-black gloves. The reason for this was that Jimmy had trouble drawing hands. Hands scared him. Fingers came out looking like bananas or blades of grass blowing in the wind. But he could draw a pretty good fist if it was inside a thick black glove, so thick that Jimmy could avoid drawing the fingers.

None of the boys in Charley's crowd, which was the "in" crowd, paid attention to Jimmy except when Charley was paying attention to him. And then they did, too. And because they were all bigger and better than Jimmy at everything except one thing, Jimmy was made to feel more than a little special. This, thought Jimmy, was a hint of how it would be when he got to be twenty-one, and famous, and the center of attention.

"O.K., Mini-Man, what do you have for me?" Lately, that was the way Charley Beemer liked to ask Jimmy to show him his comics. Jimmy felt a little funny being called that within earshot of everybody, but he was sure

Charley meant it as a compliment. Mini-Man, after all, was his superhero. By rights, Jimmy should have been proud. So why, when Charley trotted over after a ball game, a big grin on his face, tossing his ball high and catching it behind his back, why when he called out, "O.K., Mini-Man, what do you have for me?" did Jimmy feel particularly small and squashable?

It shocked Jimmy how much Charley's approval meant to him. It meant his life. Each time Charley looked at a *Mini-Man* episode, Jimmy saw his entire future on the line: the remainder of his childhood, the rest of his life as a grown-up, everything that was going to mean anything to Jimmy till the day he died. It all depended on Charley's reaction in the next five minutes.

Charley Beemer studied every single panel on the page as if it were a question on a test. Jimmy traced an imaginary line between Charley's eyes and the drawings to see what the trouble was.

"You know what bothers me? The cape."

"You don't like the cape?" Jimmy examined the cape. It looked all right to him.

"I like the cape, how it looks, but superheroes with capes—" Charley squinted in disapproval. "You know what I mean?" Jimmy squinted back. He didn't know what Charley meant but didn't dare admit it. "I mean hoods, sure. Hoods hide your identity. You draw great hoods, really good, like bombshells. Hoods are great because they intimidate. You know what I mean by intim-

idate?" Jimmy knew. He was intimidated at that moment. "So there's a real reason for hoods. But capes? What for? They could get tangled up in them, the superheroes. They get stuck on edges of things. They're not scary or sci-fi. They're from olden times, which was great, I suppose, when you're riding a horse, but you don't see anybody wearing capes in sports." Charley went on as if he and Jimmy were two minds with the same thought. "I mean, in football, you see a team wearing capes, your team grabs the guys with capes by the capes. Sure losers, those guys, every time."

No one had ever discussed with Jimmy the costumes of superheroes with the attention to detail that Charley Beemer was now bringing to bear.

"Wrestlers wear capes sometimes," said Jimmy, in a voice that was unconvincing even to him.

Charley Beemer dismissed the thought with a shake of his handsome head. "They take them off when the match starts, Jimmy." Charley's look made Jimmy wish he hadn't spoken. "Boxers don't wear them. In baseball, they don't wear them. Basketball. Hockey . . ."

Jimmy realized that when it came to discussing capes, he was out of his league. He felt stupid. How had he gotten mixed up in a "cape problem" when all he wanted to do was make Charley happy? Too bad he liked capes. Not anymore! He now looked on Mini-Man's cape as if it had been drawn by some sneak in the middle of the night. Jimmy felt contempt for the *Mini-Man* page in

his hand. Six panels of capes, capes, capes! He scrunched
the page into a small ball and tossed it into a trash can.

"Hey, a temperamental artist!" Charley Beemer
laughed.

Jimmy laughed, too. He wasn't sure what Charley
meant, but nothing, *nothing* was worth risking his future
with Charley Beemer.

CHAPTER 9

"What does it take to get this gang moving?" Father complained.

You could depend on his using that line any time the family went anywhere. Jimmy's father was ready before anybody else. He seemed to be ready before breakfast, although they weren't leaving until just before lunch. Jimmy thought his father had been ready all his life. He was organized coming out of his mother's tummy, right on time, and he'd done everything right on time (or sooner) ever since.

Father treated time as if it were another member of the family. An abused member of the family. "You're wasting time," he would say before enough time had elapsed to waste it properly. "What do you do with the time?" he often asked, with a note of urgency in his voice, checking his digital watch, which had not only New Jersey time but Chicago time and California time and Tokyo time and German time on its jammed surface. He was always checking his watch. "Time flies," "No time like the present," "Time and tide wait for no man," "Time is money," "It's show time!"

These, and others like them, were phrases that Jimmy's father liked to offer as he waited for his family by the open front door. The hum of the running Volvo engine sounded like an alarm through the house, reaching to the bedrooms upstairs. Jimmy, Lisi, and Susu dressed in panic, desperate to be the first child outside, safe in the car with the motor running, waiting for the others with Father.

Mother, on the other hand, didn't understand the concept of time. In her bedroom, with the window wide open, overlooking the car, she couldn't have missed the engine humming its insistent drone: *WastinggasOverheatingWastinggasOverheating*. But she couldn't have cared less. Time was open-ended to her. It was there to be stretched, frittered away. "Don't put off till tomorrow what you can do next week or next month or next year" was what she thought about time if she bothered to think about it at all.

Wherever she happened to be, that seemed the perfect place, possibly for the rest of her life. If she was in the kitchen, sitting at the table reading her magazine, you couldn't budge her. If she was in the bedroom straightening out the drawers, the house could burn down, room by room, and it wouldn't occur to her to move. If she was up in the attic, bent over her drawing board, months could go by—years!—and if she wasn't forcibly removed by prodding and pushing and calling and constant reminding ("Mother!" "Motherrr!" "Motherrrr!" "We're soooo late!"), she'd remain perfectly content, while her children grew up, got married, gave her grandchildren, and died.

If there was a word for Jimmy's mother, it was "patient," while the word for Jimmy's father was "impatient." This made for real problems when they had to go anywhere. Father, who was ready at dawn, was too "impatient" to deal with Mother, who responded to his jitteriness by slowing down.

Where were they going in such a hurry? (Or not, depending on whose side you took, Mother's or Father's.) They were going to visit Uncle Lester, Mother's younger brother. Uncle Lester lived on the top floor of an old, abandoned factory on an old, nearly abandoned street at the tip of Manhattan. The factory had been turned into artists' lofts, and on every floor there lived a painter or sculptor or some other kind of artist—and at the very top, in a studio with the highest ceiling Jimmy had ever seen, lived Uncle Lester. Lester was "a brilliant but unappreciated composer," according to Mother. According to Father, he was "a fake" and also "a no-talent bum." Of course, these words upset Mother—to the extent that she was listening. So Father made her feel better by adding, "Just teasing."

Uncle Lester wrote musicals for Broadway, but they never got on. Something bad always happened to them on the way to being put on. Uncle Lester started writing musicals for Broadway back before Jimmy was born, eight or nine or ten of them. None ever made it out of his loft. Uncle Lester's loft rang with music day and night. And when he was putting on one of his Broadway musicals which was never going to make it to Broadway, he'd invite Jimmy and his family to watch a backers' audition. A backers' audition was the same as a rehearsal except Lester invited an audience with money (the backers) in the hope that some of them would invest in his show so that it could go on Broadway.

This had not yet happened, which is why Jimmy's father said on the drive in that he couldn't wait to see Lester's "new floperoo." Father was teasing again. He could wait forever. He hated Uncle Lester's shows. Father thought Lester was wasting his time and Mother's money. (Sometimes Uncle Lester borrowed money from Mother to pay the rent on his loft, but eighty percent of the time he paid her back.)

Father enjoyed teasing Mother about Uncle Lester's music. He especially enjoyed saying "new floperoo." The phrase sounded catchy to Jimmy and his sisters, so they sang it during much of the drive in. This put Mother in a bad mood, which put Father in a good mood, so he joined the chant, singing "new floperoo" louder than anyone. "Why doesn't that brother of yours admit he's a failure, get married, have a family, get a regular job, and stop having such a good time. I work hard for my money, why shouldn't he?" Father said to Mother, not for the first time.

"Lester works hard, too," answered Mother, not for the first time.

"If he works so hard, why is he always singing?" Father sounded pleased with himself. This was a new line. He had never put his disdain for Lester quite so well before.

"Singing *is* his work," said Mother.

But this was not good enough for Father. "Work is what you do with the sweat of your brow. You don't sing and dance."

Jimmy wondered what Father would think of his "work" when he got big enough to do it. It wasn't singing and dancing, but it was cartooning, which Jimmy suspected would be just as bad in Father's eyes, if not worse. These thoughts were driven out of his mind by Father's booming rendition of "new floperoo."

Despite Mother's slowness in getting ready and Father's worries about being late, they were never late to Uncle Lester's flop musicals. They were always the first to arrive. Jimmy didn't mind at all. Except for drawing cartoons, there was nothing he'd rather do than go see the shows in Uncle Lester's loft.

It was no problem to fit an entire musical, with a cast of thirty and a ten-piece orchestra and an audience of seventy-five, into Uncle Lester's loft. It was that big. And it had a balcony (which was his bedroom), where a chorus of singers could raise their voices and dancers could cavort, swinging and hanging and leaping from the balcony to the living room below. The living room was Lester's stage, whether he was putting on a show or not. It looked more like a stage than a living room—and, in fact, Uncle Lester's loft resembled a theater more than an apartment. It was certainly bigger than the tiny boxlike movie theaters Jimmy and his parents were used to going to in the malls back home.

On Uncle Lester's walls hung theater posters and caricatures of shows and stars dating back to long before Jimmy was born, twenty, thirty, fifty years ago: *Show*

Boat, On the Town, The Pajama Game. This last sounded like a great idea for a show to Jimmy: a whole show played in pajamas. Maurice Chevalier, a dead French movie star, strutted on the wall in a black-and-white caricature. He was tipping a straw hat and waving a cane. Next to him was Fred Astaire, a dead American movie star, tipping a top hat and dancing with a cane. Next to him,

Jimmy saw Judy Garland, who, even though she was old, he recognized as Dorothy from *The Wizard of Oz*. But in this picture she was tipping a funny-looking pointy hat and dancing in her shorts. All the stars on Uncle Lester's walls were dead, but that didn't stop them. They seemed larger and livelier than life, bouncing off the walls. Dead but more alive than Jimmy's teachers, his parents, his sisters, everyone but Charley Beemer. Jimmy wondered how he could possibly get that much life into his *Mini-Man* drawings. It was better not to think about it.

Uncle Lester was Jimmy's favorite relative, the only grown-up he knew who acted like a kid. Uncle Lester was thirty-two years old, but he never wore a tie and had the energy of a teenager, particularly on the days when he was performing a new flop musical. He spoke in half sentences and couldn't stay in place for more than ten seconds at a time. No matter who he was talking to, his eyes were on someone else across the room. And his hands seemed to be playing the piano fast, except they weren't, because he was standing more or less in front of you, more or less having a conversation.

And he was important. The center of attention. Everyone was saying his name, either talking about him— "Lester this" or "Lester that"—or calling him from across the loft: "Lester, where does the bass come in on this number?" "Lester, I don't know when I make my entrance." "Lester, is it all right if I change this line in the lyric?"

Uncle Lester was as much a star as Charley Beemer, but a very different kind of star. Where Charley Beemer made everyone around him calm, as if with him there, no one had anything to worry about, Uncle Lester was the opposite. The closer you came to Uncle Lester, the more worried you got; and if you came extremely close, you got downright scared. Because it looked like Uncle Lester was coming unglued. It didn't happen, not ever. But it looked like it was just about to happen. And the friends and family who came to Uncle Lester's flop shows thought it was their job to protect him. Everyone was there to make him feel better.

Even Jimmy's father. Father, who never had a kind word to say about Lester at home, did nothing but say the sort of things in his loft that Jimmy wished he'd say about his one and only son. "It's gonna be great. I can feel it." "Success is in the air."

But no amount of cheering up could cheer up Uncle Lester. He looked as if he was about to faint. The only thing that kept him from fainting was bouncing around. If he once stopped bouncing, he'd collapse in a heap.

I can't tell you what he said on these occasions. It didn't make sense. It was gibberish. "You don't think— no—well, I—if I didn't, but I did, so what's the point in going over it all, because the fat's in the fire, it is, isn't it?—or maybe not—if we—but no—but let's see how it goes—unless you think I should change it—but no, it's only a play—who am I kidding?"

CHAPTER 10

All seventy-five members of the audience were seated in bridge chairs so close together that everyone's arms touched everyone else's and everyone's knees (except Jimmy's and his sisters') jammed into the lower backs of the people a row in front. Uncle Lester, who was so nervous and miserable a minute earlier as he circled the loft chattering with "backers" (Remember? The people with the money!) and with members of the cast and orchestra, stood before the audience perfectly calm now. He looked serene, as if all seventy-five people, plus the cast and orchestra, had dropped in by surprise and he couldn't be more pleased.

Uncle Lester had a surprisingly deep voice, coming from such a small, boyish fellow. All the members of Mother's family were tiny. All the members of Father's family were large. Jimmy often worried whose side he'd take after and didn't like the evidence: Lisi and Susu were big for their ages, Jimmy wasn't. Lisi was a head taller than Jimmy, which was distressing, but not as distressing as the fact that Susu, five years younger, was catching up to him fast. Jimmy took after his mother in talent and size. Only one of these was desirable. He took after his father in looks. Not desirable at all: Father had big pores in his nose and tiny red veins in his cheeks. What kid would want to look like that?

Uncle Lester's "New Floperoo"

Uncle Lester began: "We've been working on *Robotica* for three years and we think it's ready for our friends to take a look at. Robotica is a robot, the creation of Bud, our hero. Bud is a brilliant scientist. But he has never been in love. He has never met a woman up to his standards. Bud finds that women are too demanding. They want him to stop working in his lab and go out to a movie or a restaurant. They want him to not be a brilliant scientist twenty-four hours a day. They want a boyfriend after five, or certainly no later than six. Eventually, they expect him to be a husband and, most alarming of all, a father who comes out of his lab and plays with his children and takes them to the zoo and the circus.

"Bud doesn't want to end up like a lot of his scientist friends who fell in love and that was the end of their endless days and nights in the lab. Their wives made them get out of their lab clothes and get haircuts and wear suits and even tuxes and go to dinner parties and go dancing and have what their wives called 'a good time.' But dinner parties and dancing weren't Bud's idea of a good time. Not to mention wasting hours of the day with a wife and kids who insist you do things with them. That was Bud's idea of a nightmare.

"So Bud went into his lab and invented Robotica. Robotica was the perfect female. She was tall and blond and beautiful as a movie star and had the softest skin to touch—except it wasn't skin, it was latex. Because Robotica was a cyborg. A robot. And Bud programmed her to say 'Yes, dear'; 'Whatever you like, dear'; 'You know best, dear'; 'Stay in the lab as long as you like, as late as you like, I'll be home patiently waiting.' She didn't want anything from Bud, anything at all. And all Bud wanted from Robotica was her undying affection. And that was the problem.

"You can program cyborgs for all sorts of things, but you can't program them for affection. Affection is a feeling. Cyborgs don't have feelings. That is, not until Bud decided to go to work on creating feelings for Robotica. Why? Because Bud was starved for affection. No one in his lab told him how wonderful he was or how special, how different, how attractive, how good, how kind, how strong, how handsome, how virile, how charming. No female, since his mother, had expressed affection for Bud.

"That may be hard for you to believe, but wait till you

meet Bud, which you are about to do. You'll see that Bud is as close as you can get to a cyborg and still be human. Bud, you will see, speaks in a monotone and exhibits no emotion. He's had no experience with love, joy, happiness, hostility, rage, hatred. Never in his life has he experienced tears. Hard to believe, but I didn't ask you here to lie to you."

"I like this!" Susu said, as if to reassure all those around her.

"Bud had observed emotion. He remembered his mother had come down with a bad case now and again. And while he was of the opinion that feelings were not appropriate to men of science, he saw nothing wrong with robots having feelings. Because, after all, they are machines. They are created by man as a useful tool. Bud thought that Robotica would be a far more useful tool if she actually meant the flattering things she said to him. From her heart (which she lacked) and her soul (likewise). As the curtain falls on Act One, Bud begins construction on a heart and soul for Robotica.

"As Act Two opens, Bud is hard at work trying to build feelings into his cyborg. And why not? Bud knew he was a great scientist. Feelings shouldn't be so hard to put into a robot, they were easily available in people. Too easily. We are always referring to 'cheap and easy sentiment.' If sentiment comes that cheap and easy, what would prevent Bud from locating some, putting it in a tube, and feeding it to Robotica?

"But his best efforts failed. The more Bud failed to get Robotica to respond to him genuinely, the more he brooded over her icy indifference. Oh, she said all the right things: 'You are my man,' 'I can't live without you,' etc., etc. But she didn't mean a word of these words. Bud became tormented. He couldn't fall asleep."

Susu could. And had.

"He couldn't work. Bud *never* had trouble working! He was in a frenzy over Robotica's lack of affection for him.

"She was his ideal. Why not? He made her. But was she grateful? No. Grateful was a feeling. Was she sympathetic toward his efforts to give her feelings? No. Sympathy was a feeling. Before she could feel for Bud, she'd have to feel, period. She didn't feel, period. And the more Bud worked on her, the more he came to realize that Robotica would never feel, period.

"This drove him to drink. It drove him nuts. It drove him—if you can believe this—to *feel*. Yes, feel! Never in his life had Bud felt feelings. But as experiment after experiment failed to find feelings for Robotica, Bud found that his own heart had opened. He *cared* for Robotica. He *needed* Robotica. Bud was in love.

"Well, one morning Bud wakes up and finds a note on his pillow. 'I liked you at first because you were just like me, but now you're not anymore. You have feelings. So I'm leaving you for another robot.' Robotica is gone!

"What will become of poor heartbroken Bud? What

will he do with his new, unwanted feelings? As the curtain is about to fall, the beautiful, sexy designer of greeting cards who lives next door knocks to see if she can help her poor neighbor whose loud sobbing has kept her up all night. Bud takes one look at the girl—and he knows. Or rather his newfound feelings know. He launches into the first unplanned act of his life. He sings her a love song."

Uncle Lester bowed his head, but his eyes never left the audience. He extended both hands as if he were about to ask a favor. "Let the show begin."

CHAPTER 11

Two hours later, after Bud and Nina (the beautiful, sexy designer of greeting cards) sang the finale, "Feeling Too Much, Too Fast, Too Soon," no one, least of all Father, would have called the show "Lester's new floperoo." The last note was sung, the last chord was played, and there was dead silence in the loft. No one applauded. Then, after ten or twenty heart-stopping seconds, the entire house went berserk. Screams, cheers, bravos. Wealthy backers stood tottering on the seats of their rickety chairs and waved blank checks in the air like American flags. Lisi was beaming with an air of superiority. "He's my uncle! He's my uncle!" she shouted amidst the cheers. Jimmy cried, "Bravo!" pleased to jump up and down and act like a kid, just like the grown-ups. Susu was still asleep. She woke up briefly for Robotica's number, "Too Bad for You, I'm the Dream That's Come True." She said a very loud "Shhh" and slept soundly through the rest of the show, including three vigorous, floor-stomping dance numbers.

"It's a hit!" "It's a hit!" "It's a smash hit!" "Smash" and "hit" were the two words that swept back and forth across the loft. Everyone, even strangers to Uncle Lester, felt a sense of pride, felt a part of his triumph, felt like privileged members of a secret society. In a matter of months, what they alone knew would be known to the world: Uncle Lester had composed a masterpiece!

In less than two hours, the small world of Jimmy's family had turned topsy-turvy. Something had changed —Jimmy couldn't tell exactly what—to make Father and Mother behave so oddly all the way home. Mother was silent, but her silence was different from any of the many Mother silences Jimmy was used to. This silence was full of wonder, it seemed to shine. Yes, in the darkness of the car ride home, Mother's outline shimmered with an inner light brought on by her silence. And it was this inner light that spoke to Jimmy. It said: "Didn't I tell you that someday we'd all be proud of your Uncle Lester? Now, like all those famous posters on his wall, he has stepped into legend!"

Father, who usually made fun of Uncle Lester on the way home, was also silent—but more noisily so. He kept clearing his throat, as if he was getting ready to say something. It never got said. What got said instead was GRMMMMPH and HMMHMMHMMHMM. Seated as he was just behind Father, Jimmy noticed that his shoulders were sagging and that he seemed to be holding on to the steering wheel for all he was worth. At one point, he pulled over to the side of the road and asked Mother to drive. He huddled right up next to her and began to sing in a voice that gurgled with woe, "Feeling Too Much, Too Fast, Too Soon."

He turned to his children and, in the same gurgly voice, said to each of them: "How you doin'? You doin' O.K.? Lisi? Jimmy? Susu?" He turned to Mother and said, "You put up with a lot. Don't think I don't know it." He didn't say anything else for a long time, but just before they drove up the short driveway into the garage, he broke into another one of Uncle Lester's new hits, "You Show Me Your Soul, I'll Show You Mine." But before he got very far, his voice cracked like a teenager's and went silent. No one knew what to say or do, except Susu, who asked, "Daddy, are you catching the flu?"

CHAPTER 12

Father came down the cellar stairs slowly, one step, then another, then another, as if he had a broken leg. There was only one chair in the cellar, a kitchen chair that Mother allowed Jimmy to have for his inner sanctum. His drawing board was in his lap with a new *Mini-Man* page on it. He had to finish it by tomorrow for Charley Beemer. Other *Mini-Man* pages were scattered face up on the cement floor, but Father didn't notice them. He was looking away. He was looking at the furnace and then the washer and then the dryer. He ran a hand across the overhead pipes. He did all these things slowly, carefully, as if there was a right order to do them in before he was permitted to look at his son. He must have thought he made the wrong impression towering over Jimmy, so he sat on his haunches, leaning forward a little, like a Met waiting for his turn at bat. He shifted his height until he was at eye level with his son. His voice, when he finally spoke, was so low it could have come from inside the furnace behind him.

"I like to think I was doing the best job of being a father to an artistic boy I could," Father began. For no reason that he understood, Jimmy was scared. "I'm not an artistic man," Father continued. "I don't know much about artistic people, but I know what I like. And I don't like them. Most of them. They put on airs. I'm average and I like being average, and they are not and they like being that way, and I don't have a problem with that, except when they put on airs, and most of the ones I've come across do. I'll tell you the truth, I've never liked your Uncle Lester. He put on airs. Not as much as some I've met, but there it is. I never let you and your sisters know how I felt because it would upset your mother.

"I thought Uncle Lester was a no-talent bum who should go out and get a real job like a real man. I guess this must come as a surprise to you. I guess I didn't think artists, so-called artists, were real men. It's more of a woman's job. Like your mother, who's artistic, and it makes me proud. It's a woman's job. I'm talking a blue streak. Women artists. That made sense to me. But men artists. Like that Andy Warhol. I can draw a better soup can with my eyes closed.

"And that's what I thought of your Uncle Lester. A phony-baloney. And that's what I thought you were going to grow up to be . . ."

Father placed his large hands over his face as if to plug

his mouth, which had never, in all of Jimmy's life, been known to chew on so many words. Jimmy didn't know what was going on, but whatever it was, he didn't trust it. He had never seen Father hide his face in his hands. Was he crying, or trying to figure out what to say next? The one thing certain was that Jimmy didn't want to know. He was scared. His world tilted off balance. This was a completely different father. Closer to the father he had always wanted in some ways—but in other ways not. His Indiana Jones of a father didn't talk this much. But he didn't have to. He and Jimmy understood each other.

Jimmy was used to women talking, but not men. At the dinner table, Mother and Lisi could talk your head off, while Father held his remarks to a few one-liners: "Don't get too big for your britches"; "Life's too short"; "I'm not gonna waste my breath on that subject." Until that moment, Jimmy had never heard Father waste his breath on any subject except the Mets. And, every now and then, Uncle Lester. How in the world could Father say he had kept his dislike of Uncle Lester secret? Everyone in the family, including Mother, had heard him say "new floperoo" and "Why doesn't he go out and get a real job?" fifty times or more.

Father was a big man. Jimmy was used to him taking up a lot of space and using up a lot of air. But now, sitting on his haunches, with his head in his hands, he took up very little space. He looked not much bigger than Mother. But he still used up a lot of air, including Jimmy's share. Jimmy had trouble breathing.

Father looked up, and he wasn't crying, but his eyes were red. "Feeling too much, too fast, too soon." Father half said it, half sang it in that strangled voice he'd had in the car going home. He stood up and walked to the cellar stairs, his head bowed, his shoulders at a funny angle, as if they didn't quite hook into his body. His mussy head of hair brushed against the overhead pipes. He turned to Jimmy to say something, and Jimmy was ashamed to catch himself thinking, "No more, please!"

Father's last words before shuffling forlornly upstairs were "I wish my old man had been able to talk to me this way."

And he was gone. The door clicked shut at the top of the stairs. And what did Jimmy think after all this? He thought, with a trace of anger, "He didn't ask to see *Mini-Man.*"

At dinner that night, during the tomato soup, Father asked everyone how they felt. This was really peculiar. Father was not a man to ask questions. And yet in the car he had asked, "How you doin'?" And now this. One by one, he went down the length of the table, quietly asking his question. Ordinarily, Mother and Lisi didn't need any excuse to talk, but all through the meat loaf, mashed potatoes, and peas hardly a word was spoken.

Father took the prolonged silence as a sign that everyone was waiting to hear from him again. During Apple Brown Betty and milk for the kids and decaf for the grown-ups, he cleared his throat and cleared it again, and when it was finally cleared to his satisfaction, he started to speak. He said it was time that everyone stopped having fun at Lester's expense and gave him the credit he deserved, and that, believe it or not, there was a lot of Bud, the scientist, in Father. And that he, for one, took pride in Lester's achievement. "Genius" was the word he used a couple of times, and each time he used it, Mother's eyes watered. Anyhow, Father went on: "No matter how successful or famous Lester becomes, no one's closer than family." So it was their duty and obligation to give him their whole-hearted support in the tough times that lay ahead, "because putting on a Broadway show is not all fun and games." He said this with a certain knowingness, as if he were an authority on whatever wasn't fun and games. Finally, Father announced that he had invited Lester over on Saturday for the purpose of presenting him with a check for $5,000 to invest in his musical. Father and Mother were going to be *backers*.

Mother burst into tears and fled the table, which Father then circled, hugging his children while saying nothing. Lisi and Susu squirmed under his hugs. Jimmy saw that they were no more comfortable with the change in Father than he was. When it came his turn, Jimmy didn't know what to do. He couldn't remember any previous hugging experience with Father, so it felt weird. Like all his blood was being sucked out of him. Like his real father had been kidnapped.

CHAPTER 13

Charley Beemer looked bored. He was reading the latest *Mini-Man,* and he yawned three times between panels. He looked up from page 1 twice to check out bike and Rollerblade traffic on the street. Jimmy's heart sank. Charley stopped in the middle of the page to walk over to the curb and have a conversation with one of his legitimate friends who slid up on skates. "Hurry up, get it over with," Jimmy growled at the conversationalists, just loud enough not to be heard.

The conversation at the curb took an extraordinarily long time. If Jimmy owned a watch and was like Father (before he changed), he'd have checked the time every fifteen seconds. In other words, he would have checked it fifty times before Charley Beemer finally got back to him—and said something that sent a shudder down his spine. "I think you're in a rut, Jimmy." In a "rut"?! And he hadn't called him Mini-Man! What was *wrong?*

Charley Beemer handed the *Mini-Man* pages back, although Jimmy knew he had left a page and a half unread. "You know what I've been thinking? You draw terrific, but your ideas are a little boring. I've got lots of ideas, not just better than you but as good as real comics. So what if we do this from now on . . ." Charley grinned and put an arm around Jimmy's shoulders. Under ordinary circumstances, Charley's arm around his shoulders would have been welcome, but on this occasion it had the same effect as Father's hug. It drained Jimmy of confidence and filled the vacuum with apprehension. "I'll give you the ideas, so all you have to do is make up the words and draw the pictures."

The way Charley made it sound, this was the offer of a lifetime. But for Jimmy half the fun in drawing comics was coming up with his own ideas. He didn't believe Charley when he said he was in a rut. He took deep offense at Charley's use of the words "a little boring." What was the difference between "a little boring" and "boring"? Or "boring" and "bad"? Or "bad" and "lousy"?

But what could Jimmy do? He was in no position to object. Charley Beemer was royalty! And his friend. But only as long as he liked Jimmy's comics, which he wouldn't anymore unless they illustrated Charley's ideas.

Against all odds, Jimmy had won Charley's friendship through the use of his talent. Now Charley was taking over that talent. Jimmy knew he was in a tight spot. And he came up with an inspiration, which is what often happens to artists in tight spots. Yes, he would draw Charley's ideas, but that didn't mean he had to give up *Mini-Man*. He'd draw both! And Charley wouldn't have to know. Jimmy could draw his own ideas *after* he had drawn Charley's ideas. In secret. After he had done his homework. It made for a tough after-school schedule, but Jimmy was sure that he could work it out.

"O.K., Charley, what's your idea?" Jimmy's smile was so insincere that the unexpected whiff of hope that suddenly braced him came as a complete surprise. What the whiff of hope meant was: Charley Beemer was good at everything else, why not ideas?

CHAPTER 14

You may have noticed that while I've spent a lot of time discussing Charley Beemer, I haven't mentioned Jimmy's other friends. It's not that he didn't have them, it's just that he didn't like them all that much. Even his best friend, Warren Asher. If Charley Beemer had asked him to drop Warren Asher, whom Jimmy had been palling around with since he was three, he wouldn't have given it a second thought. "See you around, Warren," he would have said, and made up an excuse like, "My mother doesn't want me to play with you anymore."

Does this show a side of Jimmy that isn't very nice? No doubt. All I can offer in his defense is that if Charley Beemer had asked Warren Asher to drop Jimmy, Warren would have said, "See you around, Jimmy. My mother doesn't want me to play with you anymore."

It was a rule with Jimmy and Warren Asher and their other friends, Billy Watson, Matthew Foley, and Freddy

Dixson, that one of the things you did to best friends was stab them in the back. You didn't do it to friends who weren't that close because they might get mad and stay mad. But Jimmy and his friends took turns stabbing each other in the back once or twice a month and always got over it (after a couple of days of pain and grief) and soon were close again.

Jimmy and his friends were friends only until a better bunch of friends came along. They hung out, having a good time, waiting for an offer.

Jimmy held the secret conviction that he was better than his friends. And they held the same conviction. Each thought he was better than the others. And each thought Charley Beemer was better than all of them put together. They would have given their life's blood to be in Jimmy's position, to be chosen by Charley Beemer and the "in" crowd.

When his friends saw this happening to Jimmy, they couldn't believe it and they couldn't stand it. Why him, who was the least of them (except for the rest)? Day after day, they spied Charley Beemer with his arm around Jimmy, poring over his comic books. I don't have to tell you how they felt. They felt stabbed in the back.

CHAPTER 15

Loud late-afternoon cries from the cellar. Jimmy, in full-throated fury, shrieking: "NO! NO! NO! NO! NO!"

Upstairs in Mother's bedroom, where she wasn't supposed to play, Susu was distracted from the surgery she was performing on one of her Barbies, whose leg had come off. She looked around desperately for a way out. It was Susu's habit to think that she was responsible for Jimmy. And that it was her job to make him feel good when he was feeling bad. But whenever she tried, she only made matters worse.

Lisi, in the upstairs bath, flicked bubbles with her toe and smiled with satisfaction. Jimmy's tantrums were rare and child's play compared to hers. Still and all, it made her feel closer to him to know that he, too, could go bananas.

Upstairs in her sanctum sanctorum, Mother looked up from her drawing table. "NEVER! NEVER! NO!

NEVER!" cried Jimmy. She was amazed at how clearly screams traveled from deep in the cellar three flights up to her desk. "Is this something I should look into?" she wondered in the distant recesses of her mind. But she was at a difficult point in the fashion sketch she was drawing and forgot to answer the question. A rule of motherhood was to know instinctively whose screams demanded attention: Lisi's always, or there would be no peace; Jimmy's hardly ever. After a half hour or so, he'd calm down.

Father was still at work, or he would have charged down to the cellar and hugged Jimmy.

Charley Beemer was responsible for Jimmy's screams.

Jimmy had been working for two hours on Charley's comic-book idea. But he couldn't get a handle on it. Charley's superhero was called Bullethead, for the very good reason that his head was a bullet with human features. Bullethead was a self-propelling weapon of death. Fast as a bullet, he drilled through walls and people. Charley Beemer appreciated violence. Blood and guts and severed bodily parts were to be drawn in gory detail, so went his instructions. Jimmy had no objection to violence, but there were bounds of good taste. Jimmy had a more delicate temperament than Charley's. It physically upset him to draw amputated heads and severed limbs. It gave him a stomachache. But Charley was insistent. He wanted to see heads, arms, and legs ripped to shreds on contact with Bullethead.

Charley Beemer was a horror-movie freak. Jimmy's comics were too babyish for him. He wanted to create comic books that would look like horror movies on the page. But Jimmy didn't go to horror movies. They made him sick. Trying to draw severed heads and limbs made him sicker. But that's what Charley ordered. And that was the problem. The great Charley Beemer had offered Jimmy friendship. If Jimmy let Charley down . . . The outcome was too awful to contemplate. However Jimmy felt about severed bodily parts, his future happiness, the structure of his life for years to come was at stake. It rested on a roll of the dice: Jimmy either came up with severed bodily parts, and thereby basked in Charley's aura as his collaborator—or he failed to come up with severed bodily parts, and was severed from Charley like a bodily part.

Jimmy groaned at the fate that forced him into such a position. The whole idea behind drawing comics (aside from the sheer joy of it) was to bridge the gulf between himself and other boys who were better than he was at everything. Comics were his way into the "in" crowd. Comics were his stepping-stone to popularity.

But here came the twist: the price he was asked to pay for such popularity was to put aside his inspiration for Charley Beemer's. It was a high price, but a price Jimmy thought he could handle, and should. As his father might say, it was "a good career move."

So he worked at it. He worked hard at it. The evidence was in tatters all over the cellar floor: hundreds of shredded drawings. All of them bad. Finally, it had to be admitted. As hard as Jimmy's head worked at giving Charley Beemer everything he wanted, his drawing hand rebelled. His fingers went on strike. They refused to draw gory flying heads and arms and legs.

Which brings us to this peculiar coincidence. To draw a good severed arm, you have to be able to draw hands that resemble hands and not blades of grass or unidentifiable smudges. Not only could Jimmy not draw hands, but now he had reached the point where his hand could not draw, period.

He surveyed the results of two hours of heartbreaking

labor. It was hard not to scream. Why shouldn't he scream? He looked down at a floor full of torn drawings of severed hands. Was the awful truth of his life now revealed? Was he doomed to be as much a flop as a cartoonist as he was as a boy?

Under the circumstances, the only sensible solution *was* to scream, rip up the shreds of his drawings into smaller shreds, kick his chair from one corner of his inner sanctum to the other, and bang his two fists on the wall, his drawing hand hardest of all.

CHAPTER 16

Uncle Lester had changed. Jimmy could not help notic-
ing the difference in him. It was the night after the tantrum, and Jimmy was not screaming anymore. He was
brooding. And while the brooding made him quieter,
inside it didn't feel much different from screaming.

Uncle Lester was a success. He had a new way about
him that spelled "success." His old way spelled "floperoo." Now, on the surface, he behaved no differently
from the way Uncle Lester the floperoo behaved. He
wasn't cocky or boastful. He didn't talk about himself too
much. But his edges looked more in focus, while the
edges of everyone near him got fuzzier. The word that
Jimmy might have applied to him, had it been in his
vocabulary, was "charisma." It meant that Uncle Lester
had become larger than life, much larger than Father,
although he was only half his size.

Only a week earlier, Jimmy believed that he and Uncle
Lester had a lot in common. Both were flops. Neither

was respected by Father. A week ago Lester stood out like a beacon in the dark, the light through the haze of Jimmy's everyday life with its every-minute letdowns. Uncle Lester was his future, although Jimmy intended to make his a better future. He would be famous, unlike the Uncle Lester of a week ago. Jimmy, too, was going to have a loft in downtown New York City, with friends dropping in from show business. Jimmy, too, would have a good time, while others, like Father, sneered at him. Jimmy's dream was to have the success that made up for Uncle Lester's failures.

But, in one shattering afternoon, it all turned around. Lester was propelled out of Jimmy's orbit. There was no question now who was the success and who was the failure.

"Another beer, Lester?" Father asked.

"Not right now, Ben. Thank you."

"Would you prefer white wine?"

"No, thanks."

"No trouble. I can uncork one in a jiffy."

"I'm fine, Ben, really."

"Pass your Uncle Lester the baked ham before you take seconds," Mother admonished Jimmy. Uncle Lester's baked ham lay nearly untouched on his plate, and yet Mother was offering him seconds when she could see, plain as the nose on her face, that it was her son's plate that was empty. Only Father's boss ever got that kind of treatment at the dinner table.

"Are you cast yet, Uncle Lester?" Lisi asked. It annoyed Jimmy that Lisi knew what to ask and he didn't. She knew such good questions! It was Jimmy who had a special artistic connection to Uncle Lester, but he wouldn't have known how to put that question into a sentence: "Are you cast yet?" Lisi made it sound so easy, as if she was already a grown-up, talking to other grown-ups. But she wasn't a grown-up, she was *acting*. She was as phony as an actress. She sounded as if she was part of Lester's show when, by rights, Jimmy should have been.

By the time he finished mumbling his angry thoughts to himself, Jimmy caught only the end of Uncle Lester's response: "—so now that the money has been raised so fast, we can go right into production."

"The money's all raised?" asked Father.

"In record time," said Uncle Lester.

"You don't need any more?" Father sounded casual.

"We've got so much I don't know where we're going to spend it all," joked Uncle Lester. Everyone laughed, which appeared to be the correct reaction to Uncle Lester's jokes, whether funny or not, from now on.

Jimmy saw Mother lean over and squeeze Father's hand under the table. Father jerked his hand back into his lap as if he were the old father. Then he must have remembered the father he had changed into, and he took Mother's hand back and smiled at her as if to say, "Sorry, wrong father."

Jimmy knew Father's real smile from his fake one. In

his fake smile, his lips were pressed so tight you couldn't pry them apart with a crowbar. Father was no more smiling inside than Jimmy was. And Jimmy knew why: he had done nothing all week but boast about investing in Lester's show. And now Lester, who had borrowed money from Mother for years (and paid it back eighty percent of the time), was too important to need Father's investment. Jimmy saw his family through new eyes. As instantly as Uncle Lester had become a star, Father had become a flop, just like his son. Father was not going to make it to Broadway as a backer.

CHAPTER 17

After Mother served decaf, the children were excused
from the table. In the old days Jimmy hated to leave,
Uncle Lester was such fun to be around. But now he
couldn't wait to get downstairs to his inner sanctum. Difficult though it was to admit, Uncle Lester had become
too much of a big shot to have fun with. The real test
was to see if he came down to the inner sanctum. Of all
his relatives who came for visits, Uncle Lester was the
only one who bothered to drop in on Jimmy. He was the
only one to say, "Got anything good to show me?" instead
of what the rest of his aunts and uncles and grown-up
cousins said, which was: "Don't you think it's about time
you were interested in *something* besides cartooning?"

Jimmy waited, with his drawing board in his lap, for
the sound of Uncle Lester opening the cellar door to the
inner sanctum. Although he was sure it wasn't going to
happen. That's just the way it was and was going to be

from now on, and he was a jerk to worry about it instead of what he should really worry about: learning to draw a good severed arm for Charley Beemer. Jimmy got angrier and angrier as he drew one lousy severed arm after the other. The problem wasn't the arm itself but those impossible-to-draw five fingers that completed the arm. They changed from looking like weeds, to minnows, to bananas. If you don't believe me, take a look.

Truly disgusting!

"Got anything good to show me?"

Jimmy was so concentrated on drawing fingers that he hadn't heard Uncle Lester open the cellar door or walk down the five creaky wooden steps or cross the concrete floor. But he was there! Like a superhero, he had appeared when he was most needed and least expected, squinting over Jimmy's shoulder as if he wasn't a Broadway star and possibly stuck-up.

"Got anything good to show me?"

Jimmy's insides turned upside-down. He had expected disappointment, and instead, Uncle Lester had arrived. This shift in reality took getting used to. He slammed a hand over the hands he was drawing.

Uncle Lester sat down on the dusty cellar floor in front of Jimmy, just as if he wasn't a celebrity. He smiled his old familiar "you and me, Jimmy" smile just as if he hadn't changed at all. "Is this a trick?" Jimmy wondered.

But even as the thought flashed through his mind, renewal of faith in Lester rang like a church bell inside him. Before another minute passed, fifteen pages of crumpled but not yet shredded severed arms were smoothed out to demonstrate the depth of Jimmy's failure. "I just can't!" moaned Jimmy, relieved to have a favorite uncle to confess to. *And* a big shot!

Uncle Lester studied every crumpled drawing, humming softly to himself one of the hit songs from his new Broadway musical. Considering Lester's triumph and Jimmy's failure, Jimmy didn't think this was quite fair, but he was in no position to complain.

"Why in the world do you want to draw severed arms in the first place?" Uncle Lester asked. Jimmy explained about Bullethead.

"I'm sorry, Jimmy, but if you ask me—well—I don't really—that whole idea—it's only my opinion, but—" And before he managed to stammer out the rest of the words, Jimmy knew that Uncle Lester hated the Bullethead idea. Jimmy was staggered. It scared and thrilled him that Uncle Lester, who hadn't met, didn't know, had never heard of Charley Beemer, would, nonetheless, so brazenly challenge him. He had taken it for granted that a Charley Beemer idea was, by definition, brilliant. And that his own rebellion and despair were due to incompetence and maybe envy.

Inspired by Lester's disdain for Bullethead, Jimmy dragged out from under a box of kitchen-floor tiles his most recent Mini-Man adventures. "Now this is more like it!" said Uncle Lester, as he sat on the cellar floor thumbing through the pile of *Mini-Mans*. He started to read and stopped humming. He chuckled, he guffawed, he grinned from ear to ear, he clapped his hands and rolled back and forth on his butt, kicking his skinny legs in the air. Jimmy tried to follow his eyes from panel to panel to spot exactly what he was reacting to, but Lester read so fast Jimmy couldn't keep track of him.

He laid the comics down carefully on the cellar floor. His eyes went soft as he stared at Jimmy. "The very, very, very, very top-of-the-line state-of-the-art best!"

Jimmy was so overcome he didn't know how to respond. Anyhow, Lester didn't give him time. "You know what I must do? With your permission, of course. I must borrow these. And run off two dozen copies on my copier. And bind them. And that will be my present to you. May I?"

Uncle Lester had asked the question as if Jimmy would be doing him a favor. And Jimmy realized that success *hadn't* changed him. He was the same old pal of an Uncle Lester he had always been. But success had changed something: it had changed *everyone* around Lester. It had changed Father, Mother, and Lisi. Lester wasn't stuck-

up at all; they just insisted on treating him that way.

Jimmy grunted, which was his sign to Uncle Lester that he could take the *Mini-Mans* home with him. "But what am I gonna do about these? I still gotta do these!" He held up the crumpled pages of severed arms.

Uncle Lester stood up and brushed his pants off. Jimmy could tell he was trying to come up with something significant to say. "You can't draw hands." Uncle Lester shrugged. "Until *Robotica*, I couldn't write a love song. For twelve years, *twelve* years, I could write any type of song—any type of song, but not a good love song." Uncle Lester looked pained. "What good is a tree without leaves? What good is the sky without stars? What good is a Broadway musical without a love song?"

"But you wrote a *great* love song!" said Jimmy, and he sang the first bars of "Feeling Too Much, Too Fast, Too Soon."

"That's easy for you to sing," said Uncle Lester. "But I struggled, failed, struggled, failed. Twelve years." He nodded repeatedly, as if he was counting out the years. "Then I got up one morning, went to the piano"—he snapped his fingers—"and in five minutes I had written my love song."

Jimmy didn't get it. "But how?"

"*That's* how," said Uncle Lester, as if that was the answer. "Some songs are ten-minute songs," he continued. "They need only ten minutes to write. Some songs need twenty or thirty minutes. Other songs turn out to be two-day songs, or two-week or two-month songs. My love song happened to be a twelve-year song."

"Oh, I see," said Jimmy, not seeing at all.

"You can't write a good song until it's ready. The way it gets ready sometimes—too many times—is you write a lot of bad songs, what people call 'failures.' 'Failures,' " he repeated, with a curl of his lip. "Ha! Every 'failure' is a piece of future luck. Because it brings you closer to being ready. To fail, fail some more, and fail again and double-fail, triple- and quadruple-fail. Fail so badly that nobody thinks you'll ever do anything else—" Lester paused. "But that's not what you think."

"It's not?" said Jimmy.

"Because you know beyond—beyond the shadow of a doubt"—Uncle Lester went on as if he had given failure a lot of thought. And why not?—"that failure is the ugly duckling."

Now, Jimmy might have guessed that failure was a disease you couldn't cure or a dark tunnel you never came out of, but not in a million years would he have guessed that failure was the ugly duckling.

"You don't get to be a beautiful swan by accident," said Uncle Lester. "The only way to be a beautiful swan is, you start out as an ugly duckling. And you get through it."

Now Jimmy understood. "Like caterpillars who turn into butterflies?"

"Exactly!" said Uncle Lester.

"Like you've got to learn to walk before you can run!" said Jimmy.

"That's my boy!" cheered Uncle Lester.

"And like, if I want to draw a good hand with good fingers, I've got to draw a hundred, maybe a thousand, maybe ten thousand bad, awful, lousy hands."

"I couldn't have said it—said it—said it better myself." Uncle Lester's eyes sparkled. He put an arm around Jimmy and pulled him close. "So—so—so what do you say?"

Jimmy said nothing. What was he supposed to say? Uncle Lester had just taught him that failure was O.K. O.K.? Failure was horrible! Everything in his life told him that Lester didn't know what he was talking about. But that was obviously not so. If Uncle Lester wasn't an authority on failure, who was?

But how could anything that made you feel so awful be good for you? Then Jimmy remembered the rest of it. Failure was only good if you treated it as if it weren't failure but normal. If you treated it as if it didn't prove what a jerk, what a loser you were.

Failure was normal? *Failure was normal?* Not for a second did Jimmy believe this. But then he remembered the hardest part: failure only worked if you went on. And on. And on. No matter how many times you failed, you couldn't give up. And that was the catch. Because deep in his heart Jimmy knew he wanted to give up.

CHAPTER 18

Jimmy approached the blackboard as if it were the out-field. Mrs. Minnafy didn't understand; this was her class-room, she belonged here, not Jimmy. She made up the questions on the blackboard that he was supposed to an-swer and did answer "correctly" most of the time. The worst thing in school was the answers. There was a "cor-rect" or "incorrect" answer in every subject except English composition, where his comp teacher, Ms. Hazeltene, pretended he had choices. But the way it turned out, they were almost always hers.

Jimmy wasn't happy giving answers even when they were "correct." Because to him the "incorrect" answer made about as much sense as the "correct" answer. The difference between them might be one digit or one dec-imal point to the left or to the right, or a misplaced state capital that belonged one or two states over on the map, up or down or sideways.

Jimmy had a good memory, but not for that sort of stuff. He could remember the names, costumes, and powers of every DC and Marvel superhero going back more than fifty years to Superman, Batman, and Captain America. Pretty good for a kid his age. But the answers he had to memorize for school had nothing to do with the questions he was interested in. They had to do with what Mrs. Minnafy and Ms. Hazeltene were interested in.

Jimmy understood the purpose of school questions: while they had nothing to do with real life, a kid had to do well at them in order to graduate and get into real life. To Jimmy, school was not about learning but luck. Getting away with a good grade by faking it or memorizing. Whichever. Memorizing seemed as much a cheat to him as cheating. Why? Because the stuff he memorized for class on a Monday he had forgotten by Tuesday. But by that time he had his good grade, so big deal. What did any of this have to do with his life?

His life was waiting for him outside the classroom in the person of Charley Beemer. The answer Jimmy needed wasn't the one he was making up at that moment on Mrs. Minnafy's blackboard. The question now driving him crazy (as he made squeaky, ear-splitting chalk sounds) was: Why should he suffer through ten thousand bad drawings of a hand when cartooning was supposed to be fun? And he was supposed to be good at it. Other kids were good at baseball. Or even school! Jimmy saw no sign of them suffering over *their* skills. Why should he be the first kid in history to suffer over what he was good at? That was the question he needed answered, not the dopey math problem he was struggling with on the blackboard. But if he had asked that question of Mrs. Minnafy, would she have an answer, would she even know what he was talking about?

"Excellent, Jimmy, much improvement over yesterday," said Mrs. Minnafy. "You may take your seat."

CHAPTER 19

Charley Beemer read so slowly it started to give Jimmy a headache. But he *was* smiling. And he was nodding his head. He turned page 1 of *Bullethead* over, eagerly expecting page 2. But there was no page 2. "Where's the second page?"

"That's all I had time to do," Jimmy said. Casually, he hoped.

"One page?"

Jimmy nodded. Casually, he hoped.

"You only did one page?" Charley acted as if Jimmy was playing a trick on him and would now come up with the rest of the comic book.

"My Uncle Lester wrote this musical"—this was the excuse Jimmy had been rehearsing inside his head, on and off all day—"so I didn't have time."

Charley Beemer read the one and only page over again, more slowly than the first time.

BULLETHEAD
WHO IS THIS AVENGING WEAPON OF DEATH WHO BRINGS VIOLENCE AND DEATH TO THE MAFIA DRUG CARTELS AND GANG LORDS?
BETTY TODD, A STAR REPORTER
I'M REALLY FED UP WITH CRIME.
ME TOO
STORY CHARLEY BEEMER
PICTURES
BOB BARRY IS BETTY'S PLAYBOY BOYFRIEND
OH YOU DONT CARE! YOUR RICH!
OUCH! YOU ALWAYS PICK ON ME!
I WONT PICK ON YOU ANYMORE! WERE THREW!
C'MON! GIVE ME A BREAK!
I WONT DATE YOU ANYMORE UNTIL YOU FIGHT CRIME!
BUT I COULD GET HURT!
YOU COWARD!
MY OLD FRIEND PROF STEIN WILL HELP ME OUT! ILL GO SEE HIM!

"You don't like it?" Jimmy gave up trying to sound casual.

Charley shrugged his mighty shoulders. "It starts out pretty good, but nothing happens. They're just . . ." He fished for the right word. "Talking." He looked again. "They're talking," he said as if what he was seeing couldn't be true. "They're talking."

"They're saying just what you told me," Jimmy said in defense of his one and only page.

"Yeah," muttered Charley. "You couldn't do it in a week?" He looked at Jimmy in disbelief.

"My uncle wrote a Broadway musical . . ."

"Yeah?" Charley didn't get it. His field was sports. It's possible he didn't know what a Broadway musical was. Anyhow, what did it have to do with his *Bullethead*?

"I'm gonna work on it tonight," Jimmy promised.

"There's no musical tonight?" Coming from anyone but Charley Beemer, that would have been a nasty crack.

"No," said Jimmy.

"You're gonna?"

Jimmy nodded.

"It's a good idea, right?"

Jimmy nodded.

"I mean, you want to do it, right?"

Jimmy nodded.

"You don't *not* want to do it?"

"I want to do it."

"Because if you don't—"

"I want to."

"Well, if you don't—"

"I got stuck!"

"Yeah, but if you don't—"

"I swear I'll finish it tonight, Charley!" Jimmy was pleading, not a pleasant sight to see.

CHAPTER 20

Jimmy stared and stared and stared some more. What he was staring at was a sheet of blank white paper. It sat on his drawing board in the laundry room in the cellar. His inner sanctum. The blank sheet of paper stared back at him in a threatening manner. "Draw on me and you will be sorry," it was saying. Not really. Paper can't talk. But that's how it seemed.

If you know some artists or writers, ask them about blank white paper. It is frightening. It scares you because it looks so white with expectation. White to signify hope. White to signify "Who do you think you are? Ha!"

And white to signify the prizes you're going to win as a result of the drawing or story you put down on the blank white sheet of paper. And sooner or later, when you can't think of any more errands, when you've gone to the bathroom one time too many, when you've lost your favorite pencil but you didn't do a good job and found it before you were ready and it's between your fingers twitching with anticipation, you touch it to the blank sheet of clean white paper. And it's over. The paper is ruined. The line you drew stinks. The prize goes to someone else. Who deserves it. Because *that* artist isn't scared of white paper.

That artist didn't have Charley Beemer looking over his shoulder. That artist drew because he thought drawing was fun, as much fun as Jimmy once thought it was. Before Charley Beemer. Drawing was Jimmy's job now. Going down to his inner sanctum was like his father going to the office in the morning and coming home after dark, with nothing to say because what was there to say about a job except "I'm tired" or "How many days left till the weekend?"

Jimmy wanted to be Uncle Lester's kind of artist, who didn't have a job. He had fun. When he drew his own ideas, he was like Uncle Lester; when he drew Charley

Beemer's, he was like Father. And his inner sanctum was no longer his hideaway but his trap.

"Jimmy!" His mother! "Jimmy, where are you?" If he didn't move or breathe, she might not find him. "Jimmy, I need you to run an errand for me!" She was standing at the top of the cellar steps, calling down as if she knew where he was, but how could she?

He was too busy to run an errand; he had his job! Quickly he sketched Bullethead on the blank white sheet of paper. Not bad. Jimmy was ready. He couldn't possibly run an errand for his mother. "Why can't Lisi go?"

"Come upstairs."

"I'm drawing."

"Come upstairs, Jimmy."

"Later."

"I need your help. I don't ask for it often."

"You never ask Lisi."

"Upstairs. Be generous, *please*." The door to the cellar closed with a click.

Jimmy didn't want to go, especially after the way she said "please." It was not a polite "please," like "Please do me a favor." It was more the kind of "please" that went "Please remember that what you're doing is not as important as anything I want you to do whenever I ask, no matter how unfair."

Upstairs in the kitchen, Jimmy's mother sat at the table reading a magazine. Jimmy came up from the cellar and waited by the door. She went on reading. "First, she's in

a hurry, and then she reads," Jimmy thought. He decided not to speak. (Maybe she forgot!) He stood by the open cellar door waiting for the right moment to back himself downstairs.

Mother turned the page, and Jimmy seized the moment, taking a quiet step backwards. Not a sound did he make, nor did Mother look up. But she said, "Wait." She said it so quietly Jimmy might have missed it. Lisi would have missed it. *She* wouldn't have waited. *She* would have gone about doing what she wanted. *She* didn't want to go on errands, so she never did. Jimmy didn't want to go on errands, but he didn't have Lisi's temper, so he did. That's what was so unfair. Jimmy took another step back.

"I'm just finishing this paragraph," said Mother in a low voice, not looking up from the magazine.

Jimmy waited. Mother finished, looked up from the page, and stared into space for a moment as if she'd forgotten what she had made Jimmy wait for. Jimmy fidgeted. His feet shuffled. By rights, he should be downstairs drawing away on *Bullethead*. He felt ready. Eager! Why was he standing here killing who could guess how much time waiting for his mother to prepare herself to speak? He pictured himself bent over his drawing board, his tongue in his cheek (which is where he put it when he drew), turning out page after page for Charley Beemer.

"The most interesting article . . . ." Mother mused, looking down again at the magazine.

"Huh?" said Jimmy, meaning, Are you ever gonna let me out of here?

Mother picked up the magazine. "About Picasso. Pablo Picasso. You know who he is?"

"Sure," Jimmy said, thinking, What is this, a test?

Mother waited for more. Jimmy groaned, but not out loud. "He's a painter."

"A *great* painter," Mother corrected.

Jimmy nodded in the same way he did when Mother took him forcibly by the hand to the Museum of Modern Art in New York and made him look. Jimmy didn't mind art if he could see it alone and decide for himself what he liked and what he didn't. But when it came to art, his mother was like his teachers. The questions she responded to were her own, not Jimmy's. And the more she lectured him about Picasso and Braque and Cézanne, the more the canvases on the wall began to remind him of math problems on Mrs. Minnafy's blackboard. If you asked Jimmy, Frederic Remington was a better artist than all of them combined. Let's see Picasso paint a cowboy riding a bucking bronc.

CHAPTER 21

Picasso's Hat

Mother smiled her pleasant but vague smile, which indicated to Jimmy from prior experience that she was settling in and that this would take hours. "When Picasso was a very young man living in Paris, he went on a holiday with his sweetheart to the Loire Valley. But I'm getting ahead of myself. *Before* they left Paris to take a holiday in the Loire Valley—this was late spring, April or May—Picasso took his sweetheart to a chic Parisian milliner's. Do you know what a milliner is?"

Jimmy shook his head no.

"A milliner is a hat shop, darling. You should know that."

"Good. A milliner is a hat shop. I learned something," muttered Jimmy to himself impatiently.

"And at the milliner's—the hat shop—he purchased a spring hat!"

"Surprise, surprise," sneered Jimmy to himself.

"For his sweetheart," Mother went on. "I'll describe it for you."

"No!" screamed Jimmy to himself. But no use. Mother described the hat. She painted a word picture. It took days. She described it down to the last detail. It took longer to describe the hat than it took to make it.

"Am I boring you?" Mother asked.

"No," said Jimmy, glassy-eyed with fatigue.

"Where was I? Oh yes, they're on holiday. And they are in love. So in love. And they idle away their hours roaming the countryside. Picnic lunches of delicious meats and cheeses and fruits—pears, cherries, grapes— crisp French bread. Packed in straw hampers, with a bottle of wine to go with it, which is typically French, although Picasso was Spanish. Am I boring you?"

"Um," said Jimmy.

Mother nodded, pleased. "And on their last day they take a boat out on the lake, and Picasso's sweetheart is wearing her hat, this very beautiful hat that she has worn every day of their holiday. And he adores her in it. In that hat, she has come to mean to him all that is fresh and joyous in life. The spirit of spring! And on their last day, on their last boat ride (Stop squirming, Jimmy!), a sudden strong breeze blows the hat off Picasso's sweetheart's head. Blows it far out on the lake. Picasso rows after it, but the hat is caught in a strong current. Picasso reaches out and misses it. The hat is carried downstream by the swirling current, farther and farther out of reach.

And then it is washed over a waterfall and lost. Lost! And when Picasso and his sweetheart return to Paris, they are no longer in love. It was the hat, you see."

Jimmy didn't see. He didn't know what Mother was talking about.

"And ten years later, Picasso is on holiday again in the Loire Valley—for the first time since the last time—and he spies a young girl picking flowers in a meadow and she is wearing Picasso's hat! Isn't that remarkable?"

Jimmy's foot had gone to sleep. He smiled at his mother and nodded his head while backing slowly toward the cellar.

"I'm not finished," warned Mother. "And Picasso follows the peasant girl (for that is what she is). He offers to buy the hat from her. But she won't sell it; it's hers now. She has worn it for ten years and mended it when it was torn. It's hers. And she is very beautiful in it. She reminds him of his old sweetheart. But Picasso is old now, and she has her own young sweetheart. And Picasso watches them picnic together and walk among the flowers of the field and dine in outdoor cafés. And he would have given his last painting to be in that young man's place, sitting in the café with the girl in the hat.

"And every year until he is ninety, Picasso returns to the Loire Valley and walks in the fields and sits in the café and waits in vain for the girl in the Picasso hat." Mother smiled sweetly at Jimmy. "Now, that wasn't so bad, was it?"

It *was* bad. Unbelievably bad. Jimmy knew better, but couldn't keep himself from asking, "Why did he?"

Mother's eyes were soft and puddly. "Why did he what, darling?" She took Jimmy's hand and held it as if they had just shared a sunset.

"He went back until he was ninety to see a *hat*? Why didn't he just go back to the store and buy a new one?"

Mother's eyes hardened. "The story isn't about the hat, Jimmy."

"Sure, it is. The hat, the hat, that's all you talked about. Every other word was 'hat.' "

Mother looked at him as if she wished he were back in the cellar. "The hat is a metaphor. A symbol. What we call 'a symbol.' It stands for love. It stands for lost youth."

"Lost youth," Jimmy thought irritably. When he was grown up, he wasn't going to be sad for one minute over his lost youth. As far as he was concerned, he couldn't lose it fast enough.

"Perhaps this story is too old for you," said Mother. "I want you to go to the store for me." Suddenly she was all business. "The art-supply store in the mall. Take your bike and bring me back a tube of cobalt blue watercolor. Five dollars should cover it, and you can buy something for yourself with the change. O.K.?"

O.K.? Jimmy couldn't wait to get out of there.

CHAPTER 22

He had been back from the store for almost an hour and already had two pages drawn. Two perfect pages of *Bullethead*. Charley Beemer would be thrilled! Jimmy had gotten past his major hurdle, the severed bodily parts. He sketched in the gross display of heads and arms and legs by placing the heads and legs in the center of the panel and squeezing the arms tight in on the edges, so that the hands were cut off by the frame. That way he avoided entirely the thankless job of drawing fingers. Here's a sample of what it looked like:

The story was going nicely, with Jimmy working in his own ideas to blend with Charley's. It remained Charley's story, no doubt about that, but Jimmy didn't feel as if he was working on a job in a factory anymore. It wasn't fun yet, but it was close. If he worked at it hard enough and long enough, Jimmy believed that someday drawing Charley Beemer's ideas might be as much fun as drawing his own.

But the problem was, he was dying of thirst. For the last five minutes he had been able to think of nothing but the taste of root beer. He could taste the taste of root beer in his mouth. Nothing prevented him from pausing in his work, going upstairs to the kitchen, getting a root beer out of the refrigerator, and returning to the inner sanctum to drink it. In theory, that was not a hard thing to do. But as much as Jimmy craved root beer, he was afraid. Down there in the cellar, he was out of sight and out of mind. But if he went upstairs, no matter how quiet he tried to be, he'd bump against the kitchen table—or the refrigerator door would make too loud a noise closing—or a kitchen tile would squeak—and Mother or Lisi or Susu would pick up the sound, identify where he was, and ask him to do something for them.

And if he gave in to them, it would be a waste of his time, and if he refused, the argument that followed would be a waste of his time. But now he was wasting his time worrying about wasting his time. So he sneaked upstairs, and Mother caught him.

"I'm afraid you'll have to go back to the store," she said. "You forgot the red."

"What red?"

"The red I asked for. You got the blue but not the red."

"You didn't ask for red."

"Yes, I did, darling."

"You didn't ask for any red. I'm not going again."

"You know I don't like you to use that ungenerous tone of voice, Jimmy."

"I'm using that tone of voice because you didn't ask for red and I don't want to have to go back for something you didn't ask me for in the first place."

Mother decided to use logic. "But why wouldn't I ask you for red if I needed the red as much as I needed the blue?"

"Because you forgot."

Mother smiled and shook her head. "How could I forget something that important?" She looked at Jimmy sweetly, patiently, but firmly.

This was one of the things Jimmy hated most in the world: an argument in which he was right and knew he was right, but which he was going to lose anyway. If you'll check back to page 117, you'll see that Mother asked only for the blue. She may have *meant* to ask for the red, but for some reason it slipped her mind. But Jimmy understood the facts of childhood: you don't get very far pointing out mistakes to grown-ups.

Nonetheless, he took one last shot at it: "You were talking about Picasso's hat, and so you forgot."

Incredible as it seems, Mother's eyes looked troubled. "I . . . don't . . . think . . . that's . . . possible, darling," she said so slowly that Jimmy felt a small glimmer of hope. It was quickly dashed. "But even if I did forget—which I don't think I did—somebody's got to go to the art store for me."

"Let Lisi go."

Mother smiled at the foolish suggestion. "You know Lisi won't go. If you go, I'll give you some extra money to buy something for yourself."

Jimmy had already bought something for himself the first time around: a set of colored Magic Markers. This time, if Mother made him go, he'd buy a watercolor brush and a bottle of India ink. Ever since Charley Beemer had gotten bored with *Mini-Man* he had been thinking of switching from drawing in pencil to brush-and-ink, because that was how real superhero cartoonists drew.

But now, although he had a good reason to go, he couldn't get over the unfairness of being asked. "Why shouldn't Lisi go?"

"This is the time she reserves for reading."

"This is the time I reserve for drawing," Jimmy said, overwhelmed by the injustice of it all.

Mother put her two hands on Jimmy's shoulders and drew him close. "Jimmy, I have so much work to do. And if I ask Lisi, you know what's likely to happen."

Jimmy knew: Star Wars. "And what good would that do any of us?"

She asked so gently, so nicely, so reasonably that Jimmy didn't know of any way not to give in. He decided to take a leaf from Mother's book and sound as gentle, nice, and reasonable as she did. "Lisi shouts and screams, so she gets her way. I don't shout and scream, so I'm nice, so what I get for being nice is: Go to the store. You tell me that's fair, and I'll go. But first you've gotta tell me that's fair."

Mother's hands let go of Jimmy's shoulders. Her whole body drooped as if under a great weight. She shook her head, not at him, not at anybody, and walked out of the kitchen.

Jimmy was alarmed. "I'll go!" he shouted.

Mother turned and looked at him so sadly his heart cringed. "I'll ask Lisi." And she left the kitchen.

Something extraordinary had happened. Something that had never happened before in the history of his family. Jimmy had won! By just talking! Not by throwing a tantrum, just talking. That was the good part. That was the part that made him feel twenty feet tall. The bad part, the part that made him feel that all twenty feet of him should go to jail, was that, beyond the shadow of a doubt, he was sending Mother to her doom.

Five minutes later, he was so involved in a complicated drawing of Bullethead blasting a battleship apart below the waterline that he forgot completely about Mother's fate. From somewhere distant in the house, probably Lisi's room, he heard loud noises that could be tentatively identified as screams. But they went on for so long and so steadily that they blended with the sounds of low-flying aircraft and street traffic and became a kind of background hum to accompany his work.

The cellar door was flung open. Jimmy knew who it was. And he knew what to expect. He was dead. Only one way existed to save himself from death. And that was, no matter what, to go on doing what he was doing, to pretend that nothing was happening. To lower his head to the sheet of blank white paper and draw and draw and draw.

Lisi was upon him. She descended the steps screaming

and stood over him screaming. She never stopped for breath. She screamed ten or fifteen **HOW DARE YOU**s in a row, followed by the same number of **YOU ARE SO UNFAIR**s. Jimmy's nose crept lower and lower to the paper until it was inches off and he could no longer see the picture he was working on.

"That doesn't look like your stuff. What are you doing?" The change of voice—still loud, but not a scream anymore—so stunned Jimmy that for the first time since she invaded his inner sanctum he looked up at his sister.

"*Bullethead*," Jimmy said in a voice so small and shaky he hoped that Lisi thought he was merely clearing his throat, and to prove it, he said "*Bullethead*" again.

"Let me see that!" There was no question that this was a command. But it was not an angry command. It was softened by curiosity.

Jimmy had refused to show Lisi his cartoons since the time she embarrassed him in front of Father. Now, however, he was in no position to refuse. He surrendered the three *Bullethead* pages. His terror of Lisi dissolved as he watched her read. He had all but forgotten how flattered—secretly, how thrilled—he was by her interest in his work. She read his comics with the same air of intensity that she might bring to her science homework.

When she finished her inspection, her rotten temper remained intact. "Do you *like* this?" she asked angrily.

Jimmy's response was a shrug; his fear was returning.

"What's with you and all this blood and stuff? And

bodies and things blowing apart? This guy's head being shoved into a ship's propeller!" Until that moment, Jimmy thought this was his most successful drawing.

"He's a bad guy," Jimmy said.

"It's disgusting! What's the matter with you?!" Lisi shouted. She was back to shouting but had not yet returned to screaming.

"I'm just—I'm just drawing it for somebody. It's not as if it's my own idea." He felt as if he had been caught cheating in class.

"You're drawing it *for somebody*?!" This piece of information astonished Lisi. Part of her pride in Jimmy was that he was an artist and she wasn't. It was the one skill he could best her at. But her idea of an artist, a true comic-book artist, was that he used his *imagination*. He made up his *own* ideas.

Lisi did not like what she was hearing at all. "Who?" Lisi demanded to know. "Who are you drawing this for?"

Jimmy knew that when he spoke the magic name his bullying sister would collapse in surprise. From that moment on, she'd respect him more and yell at him less. He paused deliberately to build the suspense. And then, with the right degree of modesty mixed with the right degree of pride, he let her have it between the eyes.

"Charley Beemer," he said.

"CHARLEY BEEMER?!" Lisi screamed. She was back to screaming. "CHARLEY BEEMER HAS NO TALENT! YOU SHOULD DO MY IDEAS BE-

FORE YOU DO CHARLEY BEEMER'S! DO YOU THINK I'M GONNA LET CHARLEY BEEMER GIVE YOU IDEAS?! YOU'RE DIS-GUSTING! CHARLEY BEEMER'S DISGUST-ING! AND HE HAS SOME NERVE GIVING MY BROTHER IDEAS!'' With a resounding slam of the cellar door, she was gone. "HE HAS SOME NERVE!" He heard the kitchen door slam. "WAIT TILL I GET BACK FROM THE STORE!'' she screamed from the driveway.

Not for an instant did Jimmy dream that Lisi would not be impressed—impressed? bowled over!—by the news that he was collaborating with Charley Beemer. She was like no other kid he knew. She was *so* weird.

He looked down on the cellar floor where Lisi had flung his *Bullethead* pages. He picked them up cautiously, as if they might burn his fingers, and examined them in the light of Lisi's rage. They looked great! The best work he had ever done!

Lisi was crazy, but that was not news to him. What was news to him was that she hadn't made him go to the store.

CHAPTER 23

Jimmy stared and stared, and stared some more. What he was staring at was another sheet of blank white paper. The last page of Charley Beemer's *Bullethead* episode, if he could only draw it. But he'd been staring down at the paper and the paper had been staring up at him ever since Lisi stormed out of the cellar.

All he wanted to do as far back as he could remember was to draw comics. It didn't seem a lot to ask, to draw comics. It wasn't as if he was hurting anyone by drawing comics.

Oh, is that so?

He hurt his father by making his nose too big. He hurt Lisi by using Charley Beemer's ideas and not hers (as if she had any). But, whether she had ideas or not, Jimmy still hurt her. And now, because all the people he'd hurt were on his mind, he'd never be able to finish *Bullethead* by tomorrow. And Charley Beemer would drop him like a cold potato. Or was it a hot potato? Did it matter what kind of potato at a time like this?

It was a lot of weight to bear on his shoulders. Jimmy had never given much thought to the effect his comics had on his readers. He took it for granted that if he liked them his readers would like them. The only thing he had to worry about was being good. And the better he got, the more popular he would be. It never dawned on him that it was possible to get better but *not* popular. But here he was doing what he considered to be the best work of his young life, and Lisi, who was his biggest booster, said it was "disgusting." Disgusting!

Father had been hurt. Lisi was hurt. Charley Beemer appeared to be hurt (or bothered, certainly bothered) because of the one page Jimmy had brought him. Jimmy was hurt when Lisi called the best work he had ever done "disgusting." And tomorrow, when he told Charley that he couldn't come up with the last page, it would be Jimmy's turn to be hurt again. Dropped like a cold (or hot?) potato.

This was not fun. Cartooning was supposed to be fun. If it couldn't be fun, why do it? If it was going to be a job, like his father's, why put up with it? What was the point of drawing cartoons when the fun was left out? Even if he stayed up all night, past his bedtime, past his parents' bedtime, and managed, somehow, to forget all the people he had hurt (including himself) and finished this last page, why go to all that trouble for a job? He wished he could come up with a good reason.

"Play with me." Susu peered up at him from under his drawing board.

How in the world did she get there so quietly?

CHAPTER 24

Tricky Bear and the Loud Monsters

"Once upon a time, there was a tricky little bear named," Jimmy began, with such relief it's hard to describe. For a while, thankfully, his mind would be off how to draw the last page of *Bullethead*.

"Tricky Duck!" shouted Susu.

"No. Once upon a time, there was a tricky little bear named . . ."

"Tricky Mouse!" cried Susu.

"No. No," said Jimmy, feeling a little better. "Once upon a time, there was a tricky little bear named . . ."

Susu frowned, going into her pretend-thinking mode. Her brow furrowed.

"Tricky Horse?" suggested Jimmy.

"No."

"Tricky Rabbit?"

"No."

Here it comes now! they both thought gleefully.

"TRICKY BEAR!" shouted Jimmy at the top of his lungs.

It was so loud a shout that it reached Mother all the way up in her sanctum sanctorum. She jumped with fright and turned over a cup of purple paint, fearing for a moment that Lisi was back.

But, down in the inner sanctum, neither Jimmy nor Susu gave a thought to Mother or to anything else except the current adventure of Tricky Bear, which Jimmy made up without the slightest idea of what he was going to say next.

"One day, Tricky Bear was taking a walk through the woods"—this was how all the stories began—"when he fell into a deep hole that had never been there before." (Tricky Bear was always falling into holes that had never been there before.)

"He fell and he fell," said Susu.

"And fell and fell," said Jimmy.

"And fell and fell and fell and fell and fell and fell and fell and fell . . ." Susu loved to do the "fell" part, and Jimmy loved her doing it because it gave him time to make up the next part.

"And guess where he landed?" said Jimmy.

"I don't want to."

"Guess."

"No, I don't want to."

"You've got to guess," said Jimmy.

"But I always guess wrong," whined Susu.

"I won't tell the story until you guess."

Susu didn't think her always guessing wrong was as much fun as Jimmy thought. "Cat doo-doos," said Susu mischievously.

"Stop that!" said Jimmy, unamused.

Susu knew that Jimmy wouldn't go on until she guessed wrong. So, grasping at straws, she said, "China!"

Jimmy grinned triumphantly. "You are sooooo wrong!" (That's what he always said.) And now, satisfied, he continued. "O.K., Tricky landed, and he couldn't see anything, it was so dark. Anyway, he knew where he landed was a place he'd never been before."

"Where? Where?" said Susu.

That's exactly what Jimmy wanted to know. He stalled for time. "He couldn't see anything. He couldn't feel anything. He only knew that he was at the bottom of a hole and that maybe he could get away if he crawled back up where he fell in from. So he crawled. And he crawled. And he crawled. And he crawled."

Susu looked at her big brother in disbelief. Was this going to turn out to be a story in which nothing happened but falling and crawling?

Her next look, which was one of betrayal, jarred Jimmy into action. He believed he had a way out of *his* hole. He let go of a full-voiced shout:

"YOU COME BACK HERE!"

Upstairs, Mother turned over another cup of paint.

No matter to Jimmy. Downstairs, he went on: "And then Tricky Bear knew where he was. He was in Loud Monster Land, where teeny-tiny little creatures lived who were so small you could hardly see them."

"Like ants?"

"Way smaller."

"Like fleas?" Susu knew all about fleas because her cat, who got run over last year, had fleas.

"Right. Right," said Jimmy.

"Boy, that's small," observed Susu.

"But they had the loudest voices in the world. Even when they whispered, it sounded like this:

"WHAT DO YOU THINK YOU'RE DOING?""

Susu giggled. Upstairs, Mother's hand jumped and she made a line with her paintbrush that wasn't supposed to be there.

No matter to Jimmy. Downstairs, he went on: "The Loud Monsters were the smallest creatures in the world. Practically. They were so small, how could they protect themselves from being squashed or eaten up by all the bigger animals, including ants?"

"Ants are insects," said Susu in a Lisi kind of voice.

"I know," said Jimmy.

"You said 'animals,' " said Susu.

"Do you want to hear the story or not?" Susu shut up. "Loud Monsters could only protect themselves by talking loud. They were so loud nobody could stand it. They scared all their enemies away. Lions. Tigers—"

"Lions and tigers are scared of noise?" said Susu. "Since when?"

Jimmy glowered at her. "I've got to finish my cartoon."

Susu clasped her hands in mock prayer. "Please! Please! I beg you! Please!"

Jimmy couldn't help smiling. If Lisi got her way through bullying, Susu got hers through cuteness. "Tricky Bear had to do everything the Loud Monsters told him. He was their slave.

'COME HERE!' 'GO THERE!' 'GO TO THE

STORE! YOU FORGOT SOMETHING, GO BACK!'"

Upstairs, Mother thought of running down to the cellar and ordering Jimmy to be quiet. But that meant interrupting her work and descending three flights of stairs. Mother hated to move unless given no choice. But she had a choice. She had a radio. She turned on rock and roll as loud as she could get it. It almost drowned out Jimmy.

Downstairs, Jimmy went on: "Tricky Bear was yelled at day and night. And he was bossed around day and night. And he had a headache from all the yelling. But he couldn't escape. Every time he tried to climb back up the hole, the Loud Monsters yelled

'HOW DARE YOU!'

so loud he got a double headache and fell back down in the hole.

"How was he going to get out of this tight spot? He got a tricky idea. He started holding his nose all the time, and the Loud Monsters thought this was weird and they said:

'WHY ARE YOU HOLDING YOUR NOSE ALL THE TIME?'

And Tricky Bear said, 'Because of the smell.'

'WHAT SMELL?'

And Tricky Bear said, 'Your smell! You smell worse than anything I ever smelled. When was the last time you took a bath?'

"And the Loud Monsters screamed:

'WHAT'S A BATH?'"

Susu burst into laughter. "They never took a bath?!" Susu loved baths.

"Tricky Bear told them what a bath was, which, since they had never heard of it, he could make up anything he wanted because how would they know he's lying? So he said, 'You get into the freezingest, coldest water for two hours and you go to sleep outdoors naked and you don't dry off and no blankets or anything and when you wake up tomorrow you'll smell like roses.'"

(Roses were Mother's favorite flower. A vase of them was kept on the kitchen table and another in her sanctum sanctorum, where she was now sitting, with a cashmere scarf tied tight around her head to soften the noise of Loud Monsters and rock and roll.)

Jimmy went on: "Well, Loud Monsters love the smell of roses, and they thought it would be great if they could smell like that (even though they didn't think they smelled so bad). But Tricky Bear made such awful faces when he was near them that they decided, Well, what the heck?

So they did it. They dove into the deepest, coldest lake in Loud Monster Land, and they stayed in it for, like, an hour or two, till their tiny teeth were chattering, and they went to bed without drying themselves and without blankets on a windy hill, and you know what happened when they woke up the next morning?"

"They died!" Susu screamed.

"They didn't die, dummy. They lost their voices from laryngitis. So when Tricky Bear started to climb up the hole to escape and they opened their mouths to scream at him, nothing came out. Nothing came out except maybe a little peepy voice, like: 'COME BACK HERE.'

"So that's how Tricky Bear tricked the Loud Monsters. And he went back home in the woods and he told what happened to his mother and father, but they didn't believe him. The End."

CHAPTER 25

For some reason, telling Susu the story relaxed Jimmy. The second he got rid of her, he sat down to draw, and the blank white sheet of paper wasn't his enemy anymore. He created in a frenzy, couldn't stop, one page, then another, the best yet, arriving at a climax that was original. *Jimmy's* idea. But he knew Charley would love it, the last panel especially, which was Bullethead standing triumphant amid a dozen or more bodily parts! (I don't dare show you these drawings. If I did, this book could never be published; or, if it were, it could be shown only to murderers in jail who had committed terrible crimes. These drawings would cheer them up.)

Jimmy was convinced it was his best work. What excited him most was that he ended up doing more than simply illustrate ideas that were someone else's, even someone as great as Charley Beemer. He didn't feel like Charley Beemer's dumb little assistant anymore, but like a big-shot cartoonist who worked *with* Charley Beemer. Teammates. Throwing the ball back and forth as if they were buddies.

He was happy. He was proud. He was exhausted, barely taking in Lisi, who was suddenly standing before him looking no more pleasant than last time. "We've been calling you to dinner for ten minutes. Daddy is really upset. What's the matter, are you deaf?" She turned her back on him and was gone.

Sneakily, Jimmy hid his *Bullethead* pages under a stack of *Mini-Mans* under the box of kitchen tiles. He was afraid of spies. No one should view his brilliant creation before his partner, Charley.

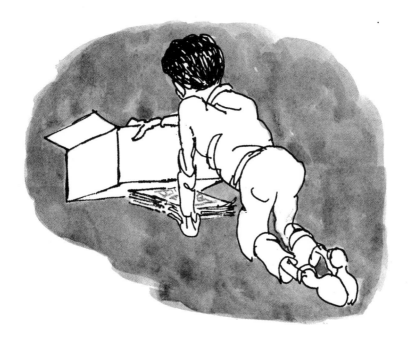

CHAPTER 26

"This isn't anything like what I told you," said Charley Beemer. He returned the *Bullethead* pages to Jimmy. He held a softball in his left hand and must have tossed it in the air and caught it ten or fifteen times while he told Jimmy, in a friendly fashion, that he had done everything wrong. Charley didn't act mad or even hurt. "I sure thought you could do better," he said with an ingratiating smile. Then his attention was back on the ball field.

Jimmy found the smile irresistible, even as he stood bleeding from every pore. "I'll do it over," he said.

Charley laughed. "I'll see you later." He trotted off with superstar grace to join the game in progress. He seemed not to have heard Jimmy.

"I'll do it over, Charley!" Jimmy shouted, to make sure there could be no misunderstanding of his generous offer.

Charley, with his back to Jimmy, threw a wave of his hand, so brief that Jimmy wasn't certain whether it was

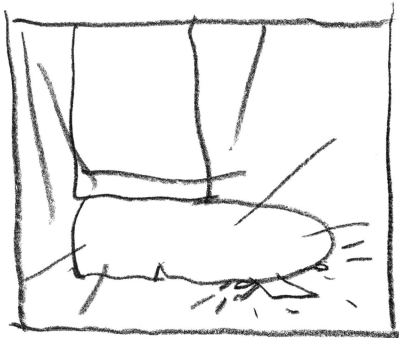

meant for him or was a signal to the pitcher to move to center field so that Charley could take over.

Apparently it didn't matter to Charley if he did it over. Charley didn't care. Charley didn't care. Charley didn't care.

Back home, Jimmy went down to the cellar, which did not feel like his inner sanctum now. He picked up a sheet of paper, intending to do *Bullethead* right this time. But no, he found that he was drawing *Mini-Man* instead. He hadn't touched *Mini-Man* in more than a week. He drew fast, outpacing his thoughts, not knowing and not caring where the adventure was leading him. He had no reaction, not even surprise, when in the next-to-last panel he drew a giant foot coming down on Mini-Man. In the last panel, Mini-Man lay squashed.

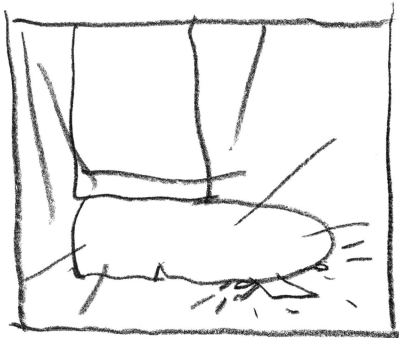

CHAPTER 27

"JIMMY!"

No mistaking that cry: Lisi, from her bedroom.

"I HAVE TO TALK TO YOU!"

You can tell a lot about who's who in a family by who comes when who calls. Lisi came only when Father called; she never came for Mother, and certainly not for Jimmy or Susu. Mother, as usual, was unpredictable: sometimes she came when she was called, sometimes not; sometimes she meant to come but forgot; sometimes she made the other person come, and if the other person didn't, she forgot. It didn't matter anyway, because she often forgot the reason she called.

When Jimmy needed Mother, he most often went to her because, if he had called her and she came, once they'd finished the business at hand she'd look around his room (or his inner sanctum, if that's where they were) and make him clean it up.

Susu came when anyone called; sometimes she came

when no one called because she hoped someone would call.

No one called Father, except for meals.

When Father called, everyone came instantly, except Mother, who came later or not at all.

Jimmy had no intention of going to Lisi's room. Let her come to *his* room. On the other hand, he wasn't in his room. He was in the bathroom. So he'd have to leave the bathroom to go to his room and yell back at her, "Come to my room if you want to talk to me!" But that seemed stupid. First of all, he hadn't planned to go to his room after the bathroom. He hadn't planned anything. For over a week, he hadn't planned anything. He just moped along, doing what came up; and since nothing came up, that's what he did.

But doing nothing was boring. Particularly if you have an alternative. The alternative, at the moment, was to go to Lisi's room. He couldn't think of anything better. He could go to his room all right, but he didn't like his room right now. It reminded him of himself, and he didn't like himself right now. So he let Lisi wait almost a full minute to teach her a lesson, then he went to her room.

Lisi was sitting at her desk doing homework. Wouldn't you know it! Jimmy said to himself. He wasn't feeling friendly. They hadn't actually made up since their last argument, but they seldom made up officially. They just forgot about the argument and went on. More times than not, they went on to have good times with each other.

But not this time. This time was different. It was so different Jimmy couldn't imagine what Lisi could possibly want of him.

"Why aren't you drawing?"

Jimmy was taken by surprise. "What do you mean?"

"What do you mean, what do I mean?"

"I don't know what you're talking about."

"You know very well."

"No, I don't."

"Yes, you do."

Four more rounds of this and they were ready to move on to another level.

"Mom says you haven't been down in the cellar for two weeks."

"Mom doesn't know everything."

"Have you?"

"Mom's not around all the time. She's upstairs in the attic. How does she know if I'm down in the cellar or not? I could be down there all day and she wouldn't know."

"She knows."

"Yeah? Yeah? How, if she's upstairs doing her designs, how would she know?"

Three more rounds of this and they were ready to move on.

"So you *have* been down in the cellar?"

"Why are you so interested in if I've been down in the cellar or not?"

"Answer me!"

"So, if I haven't been down in the cellar, does that mean I'm not drawing?"

"You only draw in the cellar."

"That's not so."

"Yes, it is so."

"Well, how do you know what I do in my room?"

"Have you been drawing in your room?"

"And what if I have? Would you know?"

"I'd know."

"With my door closed? Come on, how? You'd know. Sure you'd know," he said with a heavy edge of sarcasm, which had no effect on Lisi at all.

"I'd know. And you're lying."

Even if it was true, Jimmy was outraged. "Don't tell me I'm lying! What about?"

"You're not drawing in your room. Or the cellar. Is it the Charley Beemer thing?"

Despite his best efforts, Jimmy felt himself sliding into the hole Lisi had dug for him. "What?—I don't—what Charley Beemer thing? Charley Beemer? What? What?"

The more flustered Jimmy became, the more in control Lisi acted. "Is it because of Charley Beemer you're not drawing anymore?"

Jimmy was beet red. "Charley Beemer? Charley Beemer? Charley Beemer?" He felt foolish repeating the name, but he didn't seem to know any other words at the moment.

"That's no answer," Lisi said, in complete command.

"It's none of your business. That's an answer!"

"So you admit it!"

Jimmy didn't know what he had admitted. "What?"

"You're not drawing anymore, you admit it!"

Jimmy didn't know that he had admitted anything, but he was so confused he was almost willing to take Lisi's word for it. "So what if I'm not? So what if I don't like it anymore?"

"It's the only thing you do like!"

"What makes you so smart?"

"Jimmy, it's the only thing you do like!" Now Lisi was beet red.

Jimmy was enraged. "That shows how much you know. You think you know everything. Do you know I hate it? Do you? No! Do you know I'm not going to be a cartoonist? No! Do you know that I'm no good at it? I stink! So what? You agree with Charley Beemer! I stink! I'm glad I found out so young, before I wasted too much time. You agree and Charley agrees and I agree! So we all agree! O.K.?"

Lisi felt one of her explosions coming on. She knew it was the wrong time, but she didn't know what to do about it. Still not knowing what to do about it, she leaped up from her desk. The leap must have been frightening because Jimmy jumped a foot back. But not fast enough. Before he could get out the door, she had grabbed his hand in a bone-crunching grip and dragged him out of

her room, down the bedroom stairs, and then down the cellar stairs. She looked so ferocious Jimmy made no effort to resist. She sat him down in his chair and practically threw his drawing board in his lap. By this time, both of them were terrified of her.

Lisi slapped a mound of paper on the drawing board. She picked up a pencil off the floor where he had flung it more than a week ago and held it over him like a dagger. "You *do not* stink as a cartoonist! You stink as a brother!" She shoved the pencil at him. "Draw!"

Jimmy would have killed her if he could. But she was too scary to kill. So he did what he always did when he couldn't do what he wanted to do. He did nothing. He and Lisi glared at each other, both of them doing nothing.

Finally, Lisi, who was not as practiced at doing nothing as Jimmy, growled like a beast, whirled like the wind, and vanished like a witch up the stairs.

When he saw that his awful sister was gone, truly gone, and that she couldn't possibly know what he was up to, Jimmy looked down at the paper. He smiled a little. He drew a line. Another, then another line. They all stank. He crumpled the sheet of paper and threw it on the floor. Another sheet of paper was waiting underneath. Jimmy glared at it for a long time. He was so busy glaring he forgot to breathe. Finally, he breathed, although he didn't want to. Then he drew a better line, although he didn't want to.

CHAPTER 28

Two thousand people were on their feet going crazy. Two thousand men, women, and children (just two of those, Jimmy and Lisi), standing, applauding. Applause was the least of it. The crowd cheered as if it were in a cheering competition. Jimmy's father and mother, in tears, stood teetering over the front rail of the balcony. They looked down on a weeping, swooning, deliriously happy audience. Friends, backers, friends of the producers, friends of friends, total strangers were on their feet screaming "Bravo!" and pounding their palms into mashed bananas. (Like one of Jimmy's drawings.) The opening-night performance was over. *Robotica* was a humongous hit, if audience reaction meant anything.

Less than an hour later, Uncle Lester sat white as a blank sheet of paper at the opening-night party. He wasn't moving about nervously as he usually did in crowds. He was sitting still nervously. The director of the play sat on one side of him, turned away from Lester, talking a mile a minute to one of the stars. One of the producers sat on his other side, also turned away, talking to a second producer. There were five producers, and they took turns sitting next to Uncle Lester, talking to him a mile a minute, rocking their bodies back and forth, big grins on their faces. Everyone but Uncle Lester acted happy.

And that's what it looked like to Jimmy: acting. Like a play, not real life. He sat on the opposite side of the table with Lisi and his parents (Susu was too young to go to opening nights). It felt as if he'd gone from one play to another. The first play was on the stage, the second was the opening-night party. And as wonderful as the play by Uncle Lester was, this second play was even more interesting. And a lot scarier. This laughter, unlike the laughter he'd heard at the first play, was loaded with tension. The noise was more deafening. Every voice was loud, every gesture was big, every laugh was explosive.

In this second play, anything could happen in any corner of the restaurant and Jimmy wouldn't be ready for it. It was more scary than it was fun, but a tingly, pleasant kind of scary. A kind of scary that Jimmy would remember for the rest of his life and talk about: Uncle Lester's smash-hit opening-night party.

Although it wasn't officially a hit yet. Not until the critics had turned in their reviews. "What's a critic?" Jimmy asked Uncle Lester, who now looked so bleached and transparent he could have passed for a ghost. Uncle Lester wasn't talking to anyone, so Jimmy's question went unanswered—that is, until one of the producers took pity on him. "Critics are people who write for newspapers, magazines, TV and radio, who you don't know—I don't know—nobody knows—nobody wants to know. And this minute they are deciding the fate of your Uncle Lester's play." This information came from the producer named Herb, who had such an awful eye twitch Jimmy wondered if it wasn't a trick being performed for his amusement.

A second producer, named Ira, with fingernails bitten to the quick, went on: "Opening nights, the critics rendezvous at a secret spot on the waterfront. And that is where they board a long black windowless van called the Critic-Mobile. They are all dressed in black and wear hoods. Why is that, you may ask." But that was not what Jimmy wanted to ask. What Jimmy wanted to ask was: "Why don't you stop biting your nails?"

"A critic doesn't have to be right—who can be right all the time?—but he has to be fair." Ira slid a thumb inside his mouth and began nibbling on a remnant of nail. "You can't be fair if you can be influenced. Which is why the critics wear hoods to plays. To warn off the audience from trying to influence them."

"Why, you may ask, is it important that a critic be fair?" This came from a third producer, named Mona, who had a shiny red nose, which she was rubbing slowly back and forth with her index finger. But Mona was wrong. The question Jimmy would have asked, if he had the nerve, was: "Why do you rub your nose when you only make it redder?"

"A critic has to be fair," said Mona, talking fast and rubbing slowly. "Because no matter what an audience says about a play before it opens, they will say only what the critics say afterwards. If the critics say, 'This show is a laugh riot,' audiences will laugh their heads off. If the critics say, 'This is the best play in the English language since Shakespeare,' audiences will leave the theater saying: 'I could be wrong, but if you ask me, this is the best play in the English language since Shakespeare.'" Mona stopped rubbing her nose. "You've heard of Shakespeare?"

Jimmy nodded. "Great like Picasso."

The fourth producer, whose name was Fred, picked up the story. "But if all the critics like the show except one, and that one is the critic from the most important newspaper in New York . . ." A muscle in Fred's cheek throbbed.

"Vernon," the four other producers said in unison. The name resounded like an electric-guitar chord.

"Then it's goodbye, show." The muscle in Fred's cheek hopped like a frog.

"And the people who already saw the show and loved it will be ashamed to say so," concluded the fifth producer, Mabel, who wore a big smile on her face that had no connection to anything she said. "They may whisper in the privacy of their homes, alone in bed at night, 'I don't think it was that bad,' but never in public."

"Why, you may ask," Mona cut in. But that wasn't even close to what Jimmy had in mind to ask. "Because they're too scared of making fools of themselves," Mabel and Mona finished in unison.

The question Jimmy would have asked if he had known how to put it into words was: "Is this another one of those grown-up things that I'm not going to understand until I get to be old like you?" He couldn't believe that he had heard the producers correctly. But if he had, then in an hour or so a man named Vernon would decide whether Uncle Lester's show was a hit or a flop.

And Uncle Lester continued to do what he'd been doing all evening, which was nothing. He stared high over the party's head, as if he had X-ray vision like a superhero and could see through the ceiling to the sky.

Jimmy looked up, too, thinking it would please Uncle Lester if he joined him in staring. But all there was to stare at was a blank, boring ceiling—not nearly as interesting as the ceiling of the theater that Jimmy had spent half the show staring at.

Not that he hadn't loved *Robotica*. *Robotica* was great! So what if he had fallen asleep during the second act? He was a kid, up way past his bedtime. Besides, he'd already seen it performed in Uncle Lester's loft, where, if the truth must be told, he liked it better because it was played inches away, not on a stage so distant from his balcony seat that the actors looked smaller than dolls.

So he spent much of the second act (when he was still awake) studying the ceiling of the theater, which was a lot closer to where he sat than the stage was. In the darkened theater, the ceiling seemed alive! Refracted lights and shadows from the stage zipped and flickered across its gilded surface like sprinting athletes. Jimmy imagined another play taking place up there, set to Uncle Lester's music. But with supercharacters who leaped and fell and rose and fought and fell and bounced and rose and ran miles around the gilded, darkened, vaulted ceiling, this mob of shadows performing dizzying acrobatics, all in time to Uncle Lester's wondrous sounds.

Now, as he sat at the opening-night party, he felt far away from it all, as if he were one of those supershadows he had imagined, observing the party from the ceiling of the theater.

As a supershadow, he looked down from on high and saw the still and silent Uncle Lester. Around him circled the noisy celebrants, raising glasses, slapping backs, kissing, hugging, moving so fast Jimmy's head became dizzy with the whirl of it. People lost definition, the crowd became a blur. His father and mother and Lisi were part of the blur. And at the center of the blur was Uncle Lester, the only one in focus. But wait, it wasn't Uncle Lester, it was a robot. That's how it looked to the supershadow on the ceiling as Jimmy closed his eyes and fell asleep.

CHAPTER 29

When Jimmy awoke, the restaurant was empty except for Father, Mother, Lisi, and Uncle Lester, who hadn't moved. Jimmy was still half asleep and couldn't make sense of what Father, who spoke in a whisper, was saying. Mother and Lisi did not try to speak, because they were crying. It looked spooky, like someone you loved had died in the middle of the dirty plates and soiled linen. Jimmy understood only bits and pieces of what Father said, like "It's one man's opinion," "Let *him* try to write a show," "Everyone loved it."

Uncle Lester was, if anything, more still than before. He had a peculiar vacant expression that made his face look like it had been turned inside out and was hiding.

Jimmy didn't remember much about the drive home except that it was in silence. It seemed as if they were driving forever through an unlit tunnel. And he didn't remember much about going to bed, except the house felt like an unfamiliar, strange, and empty box. And he didn't remember falling asleep except for his last thought, which was his first thought on waking the next morning: "I don't want it to be tomorrow."

But it *was* tomorrow. And Jimmy was out of his room when everyone was still asleep. And he was down in his inner sanctum for the first time in weeks. And he was drawing like crazy, drawing as if he would never stop. He was drawing his new supercharacter, the one he must have dreamed up in his sleep, because why else would he wake with such bounce, jump out of bed without knowing why, and start drawing without knowing what?

And this is what.

CEILING MAN
FROM THE HIGHEST MOUNTAIN IN ANCIENT TIBET
THE MAN IN THE CEILING
LOOKS DOWN ON CRIME AND EVIL WHERVER IT LURKS ....
POSSESSER OF SUPERNATURAL POWERS. FRIEND OF THE OPPRESSED HE FIGHTS THE CRIME AND CORUPTION OF THIS WORLD!
entirely written and illustrated by Jimmy Jibbett

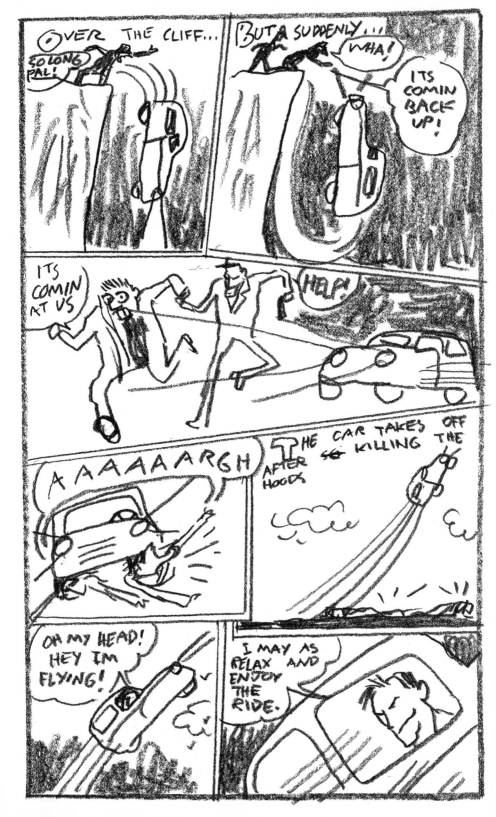

THIS LOOKS LIKE TIBET!
A PALACE ON TOP OF MT. FUJIYAMI!
ANYBODY HOME?
ANYBODY HOME?
ANYBODY HOME?
SOME ECHO!
ANYBODY HOME
THIS BEATS ANY HOTEL IVE EVER BEEN! WHAT A BEDROOM!
NEXT DAY..
WOW WHAT A BREAKFAST! THANKS WHOEVER YOU ARE.
DR ALLEN ROGERS..
A SUPERNATURAL VOICE IS CALLING ME UP THE STEPS BUT WHERE?
TO THE HIGHEST TOWER! 10,000 STEPS!
PHEW! GOOD THING I RUN THE MARITHON!

AT LAST! HE REACHES THE SKY DOME!
WHA-? THERE'S A MAN IN THE CEILING!
DR ALLEN ROGERS I AM THE CEILING MAN! YOU ARE HERE AT MY COMMAND!
I SEE FROM MY GREAT HEIGHT ALL EVIL ALL OVER THE WORLD THEN I SEND SKY WAVES TO MY AGENTS AND THEY FIGHT CORUPTION FOR ME BECAUSE DR ALLEN ROGERS IT IS MY FATE TO NEVER LEAVE HERE!
WHY SEND FOR ME, CEILING MAN?
I HAVE A DISEASE! I WILL DIE SOON IF YOU CANT CURE ME!
THE CIELING MAN BRINGS DR ALLEN UP THERE WITH HIS POWERS.
IM SORRY I DONT KNOW THIS DISEASE!

CHAPTER 30

Mother was a wreck. Father was being strong, but he, too, was a wreck. Uncle Lester was coming to dinner. "We must all be upbeat," said Father. Mother sobbed. Lisi glared at Mother. She thought she had a right to expect more positive behavior from a parent. It was her opinion that Uncle Lester should have shot all the critics dead. This opinion was expressed loud and often since *Robotica* had closed after a mere five performances on Broadway.

After the reviews, which weren't great but weren't bad, except for the review in the most important paper in New York, which was so bad Mother couldn't think of it without going to bed, and Lisi couldn't think of it without shouting the house down (and you can imagine what that did to everyone's spirits), Jimmy hid out as much as he could in his inner sanctum. The image of Uncle Lester at the party would not leave his mind: Lester staring up

at the ceiling as if he wished he could fly through it. Not
that Jimmy really knew what Lester was thinking. No one
did. No one could. Lester had disappeared.

On the day after opening night, he vanished. Where, no
one knew. "The Virgin Islands," Father guessed. "Paris,"
Mother guessed. Jimmy's guess was Tibet, though he
wasn't going to tell anyone; he was protecting Lester's
secret.

For three weeks the only sign of Lester's existence was
the voice on his answering machine which said: "I am
not here. I am sorry. I am more sorry than you can know.
I truly apologize. To one and all, I apologize. I'm so
sorry. So very sorry." And there followed twenty-five more
"sorry"s until the beep.

Mother and Father called his machine every day. They
left cheerful, upbeat messages which sounded stiff from

Father (he read from notes) and sounded worse from Mother. It defeats the purpose of an upbeat message when it's said in sobs.

After the fatal opening night, Father gathered the family around and said the following: "This is a lesson for us all. You never know. You think you know. Sometimes you *do* know. But lots of times—and this is one—you don't know what you think you know. Because life is full of ups and downs." And then Father went on to talk about his own ups and downs. Many more than his children had realized. In fact, by the time he had finished his talk, Jimmy was staggered by the number of times Father had expected promotions and not received them, expected raises and been turned down, expected assignments only to see them go to someone less deserving.

Father's talk cheered up no one, including Father. To Jimmy, who had thought the world was a perilous place only for boys who couldn't play baseball, Father's speech was truly demoralizing. Mother did no better. Rather than call everyone together (this was not her style), she sought out each child in his or her room and, adjusting for each one's age, said more or less the following: "The first thing to remember is that we have each other. And your Uncle Lester. And he has us. And that makes us proud. We have no right to ask for more. Because when we don't get exactly what we expect out of life—and who does? Not even Picasso. But unlike Picasso, we're all together. And what we learn when we're all together is that individual disappointments don't hurt nearly as much. Because we can be the most famous and successful person on the face of the earth, but without good health and a family to share it with and a roof over our heads— So let's put our troubles behind us."

But no one believed a word of what Mother said, because of how she looked, which was heartbroken.

Uncle Lester arrived an hour late and not alone. He stepped out of his rental car and opened the back door.

Out of it bounded a seven-months-old but already enormous sheepdog. "No, Vernon!" Uncle Lester shouted, as the man-sized puppy bounded up the driveway and knocked Susu sprawling. Susu screamed in terror. Uncle Lester bounded up the driveway, as gangly as the puppy. He cried: "Bad Vernon! Bad Vernon!" He wrestled the dog off Susu. Her face and blouse were sopping wet from the sheepdog's rapid-fire tongue. Next, the great dog charged past the downed Susu into the house. Crash! went the hall table, sending half a dozen pictures of the family flying. Smash! went Mother's favorite vase. Slobber! went Vernon as he found his way into the kitchen and devoured the hearts-of-artichoke appetizer. There was no controlling him and no complaining to Uncle Lester. How could Mother or Father say to

a loved one who had been through a disaster such as his, "I'm sorry, but you can't bring your dog into the house."

Vernon was everywhere at once, and where he landed he gnawed and slobbered. Chairs and tables were over-

turned; dishes, glasses, and silver went spinning off the dinner table, which had to be reset twice. "No problem," whimpered Mother. "Bad Vernon!" barked Uncle Lester, not looking or sounding angry. His face, which was ghostly white, had no expression. His voice, when he spoke (which was seldom), was a monotone. For much of the evening, he had little to say but "Down, Vernon!" and "Bad Vernon!"

So as the family sat down to dinner, the mood, which should have been a "let's cheer up Uncle Lester" mood, had turned into a "this dog is destroying our home, but no one mention it" mood.

All the weeks of pity for Uncle Lester ended within half an hour of Vernon's appearance. What could Uncle Lester have had in mind by bringing such a large, untrained, and unruly puppy to such a small house? Mother no longer acted heartbroken. She acted furious-but-not-showing-it. Besides his other sins, Vernon had blundered into her sanctum sanctorum and chewed up her precious paintbrushes. Mother served dinner by falling back on her old big-sister habit of prodding Uncle Lester on how to eat. Father gave up trying to be upbeat and tried merely to avoid making mean-spirited cracks about Lester's career in the theater. No more kowtowing to Lester, the superstar.

Despite the sense of unease at the table, they were able to dine in peace because Susu, who fled to bed early, was behind her closed bedroom door acting as a decoy. Vernon was upstairs, pawing at her door, hurling his body against it, trying to break in. His barks were loud enough to be heard in the next county.

"Where'd you get him?" asked Father, who was barely heard over the barking. Dinner discussion was about the dog and nothing else. No one asked, "What are you going to do now, Lester?" No one asked, "Where did you disappear to, Lester?" No one asked, "What have you learned from your newest and worst failure, Lester?" No one cared. Maybe they would care again when Uncle Lester had taken his awful dog home with him.

"Where'd you get the name 'Vernon'?" Father asked.

Jimmy could not help but turn away—into Mother's hard stare, which penetrated down to his socks. She was sending him a message. The message read: "Don't you dare tell." If she'd only sent the message to Lisi, she would have done better.

Lisi blurted, "Isn't that the name of that stupid critic who—" Before Lisi could get beyond "who," Uncle Lester leaped from his chair, ran to the entrance of the dining room, and shouted upstairs: "Bad Vernon! Down, Vernon!"

By the time coffee was served, the exhausted Vernon had fallen asleep outside Susu's door. His snores echoed throughout the house. Over coffee, Uncle Lester was finally asked, and answered, questions about his career. In dribs and drabs, he let it be known that within a month he would be on his way to London for a British production of *Robotica* at the prestigious National Theatre. This was wonderful news, but not the way Uncle Lester told it. He spoke so quietly, in such a dreary monotone, that he might as well have said, "Within a month, I am taking out the garbage." And he had more good news, although it was hard to tell by his manner. On his return from England, he was going to Hollywood to compose a score for a new animated full-length Walt Disney cartoon, *Rapunzel*. To Jimmy, this was far more exciting than a hit Broadway musical. But you couldn't tell that from Uncle Lester's presentation of the facts. He sounded far more animated talking about his dog than talking about Disney.

CHAPTER 31

Uncle Lester had managed to squeeze his sheepdog into the backseat of his rental car and returned to the house to say his goodbyes. His goodbyes were said in such a dead and low voice that they could hardly be told from his hellos. Out of their need to have the evening done with, Father and Mother continued to do most of the talking, and what they said made no sense at all. It amounted to "Jabber jabber jabber jabber," to which Uncle Lester replied, "Mumble mumble," to which they responded with louder and more urgent "jabber"s. By that hour of the evening, what all their jabbering amounted to was: "Go home this minute, Lester, or we will start screaming!"

Jimmy, who had said next to nothing all night, had a plan. He had been working on this plan for two and a half weeks, going to the school library every afternoon, studying and crudely copying from certain "how to" books. He was nervous about his plan, certain it would fail, but just as certain that he must make an effort to pull it off.

But now the evening was over and his effort had not begun. Somehow, the events of the evening (actually, the non-events)—Mother and Father's fidgetiness, Uncle Lester's ghostliness, Vernon's hugeness—had made him despair of making his effort. Then, at the last moment, when Uncle Lester was all but out the door and into his car, he turned and spoke to Jimmy directly for the first time. "Still cartooning?" he asked in his new dead voice. Jimmy could tell that he was only asking to be polite. No one, not Mother, not Father, not Lisi, not Susu, certainly not Vernon or Uncle Lester, wanted the evening to continue. "I have something special to show you downstairs," Jimmy said, with rising fear and expectation. Father groaned. Mother sobbed. Lisi growled. Vernon barked. Uncle Lester said nothing.

Thirty seconds later, Jimmy had him down in his inner sanctum, although it was clear that Uncle Lester didn't want to be there. But that was all right, since it was clear that he didn't want to be anywhere else, either.

"This is my new superhero, which I got the idea for from your opening night, so I'm giving it to you." Jimmy handed Uncle Lester his new comic book.

Uncle Lester didn't seem all that interested. "Thanks. I'll read it when I get home," he said in his new dead voice. From outside came the sound of Vernon barking.

Jimmy took a deep breath. He didn't believe what he actually said next. "You have to read it now."

Uncle Lester didn't seem to take this as unusual. He gave a short, inexpressive jerk of his head, stared into space for a long moment, and, having no other choice, began to read Jimmy's new comic.

IS HE DEAD?
NO— BUT HES BLOWN TO PIECES!
THE BOOMER TRIUMPHS! HA!
THE CEILINGMAN SEES ALL!
BRAD CAN BE SAVED BY MY SPECIAL OPERATION 64X! BUT I CAN NOT LEAVE HERE! MINUTES COUNT! LUCKY MY AGENT DOC JONES IS AT THE GAME!
THROUGH THE MAGIC OF THE MAN ON THE CEILING'S SKY WAVES, DOC JONES DOES A MIRACLE OPERATION!
EASY DOES IT! ITS LIKE A JIG SAW PUZZLE!
THE BOOMER WILL KILL DOC JONES FOR THIS!
A MONTH LATER...
THE WORLD SERIES IS TO-NIGHT BUT I WILL NEV-ER WALK A-GAIN!
YOU GOT TO TRY BRAD!

CHAPTER 32

"Thank you," said Uncle Lester in his awful new voice. "I want to tell you how much I like this, even if I sound as if I don't. That's because this is how I sound now. I appreciate your trying to make me feel better. But don't bother.

"You try and you try and you try. And then you stop. You can't try anymore because the pain is not worth it. So you do the things that aren't bad things, but the things you don't care about. Then if they fail, no big deal. And if they succeed? No big deal either way. Maybe you don't remember—why should you?—but when you couldn't draw hands, I told you that failure was just another way of learning. That's nonsense. I want you to grow up smarter than I was. So here's what I've learned from my failures: If you don't at once succeed, you'll never do better, so give up."

Uncle Lester's voice was so low that it seemed to come

out of his feet, which began to move toward the cellar steps. "Uncle Lester," said Jimmy, and he handed him an eight-by-ten manila envelope.

"No more comics," said Uncle Lester, coming as close to expressing emotion as he had all evening.

"It's important," insisted Jimmy. Uncle Lester looked toward the steps as if he might make a run for it. "Uncle Lester," repeated Jimmy with such resolve that Lester saw that he had no choice but to take the envelope and open it and examine its contents. This he did.

Mother and Father got tired of waiting by the front door for Uncle Lester to return from the cellar and take his dog home. Lisi had gone upstairs to bed some time ago. "See what's keeping them," Mother said.

"He's *your* brother," Father said.

"You're better at this than I am," Mother said.

"This is a bad time to lie to me," Father said.

So that's how it came to be Mother who descended the cellar steps to find Uncle Lester and Jimmy in such tight embrace that it was hard to see where one ended and the other began. Uncle Lester was swaying and bobbing like a tiny boat in a rough sea. And Jimmy was holding on for dear life so that he wouldn't be swept overboard. Mother thought she heard the sounds of sea, but they were coming from Uncle Lester: gurgling, barking gasps like ocean tides smashing against rocks. This was Uncle Lester laughing. Or was he crying? Or was he doing both? Mother couldn't tell, but whatever it was, it was coming from down deep. Had her dear brother completely lost his mind? She was about to be alarmed when Jimmy, half hidden in Uncle Lester's clutches, flashed her the biggest smile of his life.

The sea sounds of Uncle Lester broke into words which broke into song:

Thank you, thank you, thank you,
for your priceless,
for your precious,
for your peerless,
for your perfect
gift.

He sang this in a voice that was recognizably his old voice, although it warbled and cracked with emotion.

Jimmy dug his head deep into Uncle Lester's shoulder, forcing him to bring his right arm up to get a better hold. His right hand grasped a sheet of paper that Mother had not noticed before. Uncle Lester gripped it tight, as if it meant the world to him. Mother tried to see what was on it, but couldn't, so she moved quietly and swiftly down the steps to get a better look.

See for yourself, it's the last page of this book.

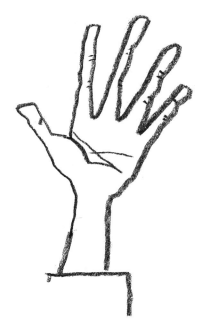